*A Teacher,
His Students, and the
Great Questions of Life*

A Teacher, His Students, and the Great Questions of Life

A Beginner's Guide to Philosophy
Second Edition

John C. Morgan

RESOURCE *Publications* • Eugene, Oregon

A TEACHER, HIS STUDENTS, AND THE GREAT
QUESTIONS OF LIFE, SECOND EDITION
A Beginner's Guide to Philosophy

Copyright © 2017 John C. Morgan. All rights reserved. Except for brief quotations in critical publications or reviews, no part of this book may be reproduced in any manner without prior written permission from the publisher. Write: Permissions, Wipf and Stock Publishers, 199 W. 8th Ave., Suite 3, Eugene, OR 97401.

Resource Publications
An Imprint of Wipf and Stock Publishers
199 W. 8th Ave., Suite 3
Eugene, OR 97401
www.wipfandstock.com

PAPERBACK ISBN: 978-1-5326-1406-4
HARDCOVER ISBN: 978-1-5326-1408-8
EBOOK ISBN: 978-1-5326-1407-1

Manufactured in the U.S.A.

On the cover, Philosophy Class by the River, is used with permission of Reading Area Community college, Reading, Pa.

Contents

Preface by Dr. Linda Lewis Riccardi ix

One	Plotimus Introduced	1
Two	What Is Wisdom?	7
Three	What Is Thinking?	14
Four	How Do We Know Anything?	19
Five	Who and What Am I?	25
Six	What's Really Real?	30
Seven	How Should We Live?	35
Eight	Does God Exist?	41
Nine	What Is the Meaning of My Life?	48
Ten	What Is the Meaning of My Death?	54
Eleven	Is There Another Life Beyond This Life?	58
Twelve	What Is Time?	64
Thirteen	A Teacher's Story	101

Appendix 141

"When we die, we leave time behind."

—LEO TOLSTOY

For my children, now adults: Lynne, Lori and Jonathan. You know I have always been a teacher in search of an audience. And for students in my philosophy classes over the years who taught me more than I ever could have taught them and who helped me to understand that an expensive, lengthy textbook is no substitute for face-to-face dialog. This is the short and relatively inexpensive account of our time together, which you kept telling me, was important. Plato said Socrates was someone who organized learning around shared dialog, asking questions until like peeling an onion, a core of truth remained about how best to live. May this little book raise more questions than it could ever answer.

Preface

THROUGHOUT THE HISTORY OF humankind, philosophers, theologians, mystics, and countless others have attempted to unravel the mystery of life. With the rise of human consciousness and individual self-awareness, the existential nature of life continues to be explored and examined from a variety of philosophical and theological perspectives. Philosophical ideas and concepts are as diverse as the rainbow of colors that make-up the beauty of summertime flowers. In postmodern *academia* theists, non-theists, agnostics, secularists, and atheists as well as men and women from various ethnicities and multicultural traditions are invited to sit face to face at the table of philosophy to engage in analytical and critical reflection in what Dr. John Morgan calls the *Great Questions of Life*. From my experience in teaching philosophy at a Community college, students enrolled in Introduction to Philosophy seem to typify a microcosm of what is taking place in the halls of *academia* today. Community college students represent a diversity of theological, philosophical, and secular thought that is commonplace in a pluralistic age. Each semester philosophy students enter the classroom seeking answers to the essential questions of life. Often students discover that they have many more questions than answers after studying the varieties of philosophical thought that exist throughout the world.

Preface

Since the study of philosophy is an intellectual and practical experience, Part 1—"Conversations with Plotimus" cordially invites students to explore the meaning of life in an easy and understandable manner through the pedagogy of the infamous character Professor Plotimus. Uniquely Socratic in his approach, Morgan carefully creates his main character—the wry and witty Professor Plotimus who introduces his "boys and girls" to a variety of perspectives that philosophy encompasses in ethics, epistemology, and metaphysics. In Plato's *Republic* Socrates tells Glaucon (Plato's brother) that education is "not the art of putting the capacity of sight into the soul; the soul possesses that already but it is not turned the right way or looking where it should."[1] Under the guidance of the articulate Professor Plotimus, penetrating conversations transform each class into a unique experience for his "boys and girls" so that they might turn and look at things in a new way. The antics of Professor Plotimus make philosophy seem rather interesting, uncomplicated, and easy to grasp while deeply compelling each time he dialogues with his "boys and girls."

In Part 2—"A Story of Time" encapsulates the whole of "narrative philosophy." Originally a fascinating tale written to help children "wonder about time," the story's metaphoric imagery and multidimensional nature moves to a time beyond time. "A Story of Time" is an amazing adventure to the utopian land of Pantisocracy as a little boy so appropriately named Adam, his doggie Sophie, and their wise new friend, an old man named Socrates, journey to the land of Pantisocracy in search of finding

---

1. Plato, *The Republic*. Translated by G. M. A. Grube. In *Voices of Wisdom: A Multicultural Philosophy* Reader, edited by Gary E. Kessler. (CA: Wadsworth Centgage Learning, 2013), 449–56.

Preface

Adam's dearly beloved departed father. Adam's journey in Pantisocracy captures the essence of "narrative philosophy" by exploring the mystery and meaning of life. It allows our minds to wonder and listen to the wisdom of the ages that life has meaning and purpose if we only loosen and discard the chains of dogmatism and venture out of our caves to experience the fullness of life not in the shadows but in God's light. Perhaps a new era in "narrative philosophy" will result as the Great Questions of Life, in its simplicity, initiates a turning around of the soul to contemplate "the brightest of realities, which we say is the Good" (Plato, 455). Come read and experience "narrative philosophy" as you travel through time into timelessness, venturing into the mystery of the journey of life.

Dr. Linda Lewis Riccardi
Adjunct Professor of Philosophy
Reading Area Communtiy College
Reading, Pennsylvania

One

Plotimus Introduced

As a philosophy teacher I know firsthand how boring and overpriced most of the textbooks are for my students, many of whom are either terrified of any courses with the words *epistemology, ontology,* or *deontological* in their descriptions or indifferent, thinking only of three credits needed as one elective for the humanities requirement. Actually, I felt the same way before taking my first undergraduate philosophy course, and I only took it because there were no other courses I hadn't taken at the deadly 8-9 a.m. Monday, Wednesday, Friday time slot. I was prepared for a long and tedious three months, bored beyond words and only hoping to pass the course and move on.

I will never forget my first philosophy class. Fully expecting rows of chairs to be lined up neatly to face the teacher, I was surprised to find chairs placed in a circle so that students had to look at one another and not the blackboard or professor. In fact, that first morning I didn't know who the teacher was or where he or she might be sitting. About twenty of us waited for someone to stand up. No one moved. It began to feel uncomfortable until someone spoke out: "Is this the introduction to philosophy course?" A few of us said it was. And we waited another five minutes.

A Teacher, His Students, and the Great Questions of Life

Thinking the class might have been cancelled, I started to get up and leave. "I'll run over to the dean's office and see what's happening," I said. I had just finished my statement when a rather short young man who looked like a student got up and walked outside the circle.

"I want each of you to take a moment and look around the circle. Look at your hands, look at the faces of others in the circle—but, most importantly, look at what's in the center of the circle." He stopped while a nervous silence set in and we wondered who this man was.

"What does anyone see in the center of our circle?" he asked. There was more silence.

"Come on now, ladies and gentlemen, what do you see in the center of the circle?"

I ventured an obvious answer. "I don't see anything."

"That's right! Why? Because there appears to be nothing there now but in the coming months we shall fill that center with wild and crazy ideas—your ideas—ones that you dared not speak out loud before, ones you have thought others never had, ones that you think would cause your family and friends to think you'd gone mad."

He obviously was our teacher, I thought, but one unlike others. He was so young. How could someone so young teach philosophy? Isn't philosophy for old men and women who know a lot?

"My name is Willard—William Wilton Willard to be precise—a name given me by my frustrated poet-mother who loved words which sounded nice but meant nothing, words some of you think are like philosophy, big and confusing and leading you into fits of confusion and frustration. But I am here to help you see that each one of you is already a philosopher and just don't know it yet. We will explore the unknowable and unscrew the inscrutable to-

Plotimus Introduced

gether. In three months, you will realize that like Socrates of old you don't know much about anything; and that, my young philosophers, is the beginning of wisdom."

Get me out of here, I thought to myself as Willard began walking around the outside of our circle. "You have already learned a few things about philosophy just sitting here. The first rule of philosophy is the first rule of life: Show up. You're here; that's a start. You've also learned about the need to sit quietly before saying anything—the second rule of life. And you've learned the third and most important lesson of life: In the circle you must look at others directly, which in our technological age is quite unusual."

The student beside me spoke softly but had the courage to speak at all. "Ah, Dr. Willard, is there a syllabus for the course?"

"No," he said; "next question?"

"Is there a text?" another student asked.

"No," he said. Each one of you is the textbook and we will create our own by the time we end. You will teach and learn from one another."

"What shall we call you?" I asked.

"Plotimus," he said with a smile. "Call me Plotimus. Sounds like a philosopher, don't you think? And by the time we end this class you will know as little as I do and be philosophers yourselves."

He pulled up a chair, adding it to the circle, and sat down. "Let's do philosophy!"

And so began my first course in philosophy; I was terrified at first, but later learned to let go of my fear and simply enjoy being in a community where I could ask the big questions, even if I hadn't the slightest notion of how to answer them. I still don't know the answers, but in being a teacher of philosophy, I am indebted to Plotimus for being able to raise the questions and enjoy the dance.

What you have here in this small volume are some thoughts and activities of Plotimus, words I recorded during our classes and attempted to put together for your enjoyment and, yes, enlightenment. No book can capture the excitement of being in his class, but perhaps reading what he had to say will inspire you. After all, as far as we know, Socrates never wrote anything. Plato was his student and later wrote what he remembered Socrates saying. So I am the student of Plotimus trying the impossible task of introducing him to you.

Plotimus divided his introductory course into eleven great questions of life. He said he chose the unlikely number because someone had already taken ten commandments and he wanted an odd number anyway. Here are the eleven great questions he wrote on the board, indicating this was the only syllabus we would use:

1. What's wisdom?
2. What is thinking?
3. How do we know anything?
4. Who and what am I?
5. What's really real?
6. How should we live?
7. Does God Exist?
8. What's the meaning of my life?
9. What's the meaning of my death?
10. Is there anything beyond this life?
11. What is time?

Plotimus Introduced

If you want these questions put into academic sub divisions of philosophy, here are what they might be: Foundations of Philosophy, logic and critical thought, epistemology, philosophy of mind, cosmology, ethics, philosophy of religion, and philosophy of science. And, of course, the question about death is closely related to the question about time; in fact, it's hard to think about our historical lives without thinking of their ends. And I am not thinking about death abstractly as if it were always something that happened to other people. Death happens to each one of us and when facing it, life takes on new depth. If there is anything beyond death, well, that's another issue.

The more I have taught philosophy the more I have come to believe that these questions are by and large most of what you need to know about philosophy but were afraid to raise your hand to ask. Believe me, I was once as afraid to ask; I know many of you who are taking your first course now or are just plain interested in learning more have the same fears, thinking philosophy is for weird thinkers. And I know many of you who have never taken a philosophy course still wrestle with some of these questions. I believe philosophy is for everyone. Listen to a child's questions before she has had them silenced by adults, and you will understand why philosophy is part of what it means to be a human being. Plotimus told us the eleven questions here were formed by listening to the questions children have about life and death, and which, unfortunately, are seldom given voice in the early years of schooling.

To be honest, if I had my way, I would take philosophy into the streets and marketplaces of our world, especially to children in classrooms, making it a public adventure—

and free. Of course, college administrators would not appreciate not having any tuition charged, but this model would be closer to Socrates than any other I know. So if you are now reading this book, think of it as a conversation we are having in a coffee shop or park bench.

At the beginning of every class, Plotimus would begin with these words (they must have struck a chord because I remember them over the years): "Okay, boys and girls, get out of your seats and stand on your tip toes and try to touch the stars above and then put your hand over your heart, because like Kant, I believe only two things are amazing: the starry heavens above and the moral law within." And then as part of our classes from time to time he would have us stand up first and feel the earth beneath our feet, then stand up on our chairs, with our eyes looking upward to think about the stars at night, and our hands over our hearts to hear their beatings so that each one of us would be grateful for breath and life and also aware of others who were standing near us. After all the years since, I try to remember what I learned and how it still resonates in me, and I am still a student of Plotimus.

John C. Morgan

Two

What Is Wisdom?

The first time I attended a philosophy class I sat in the back of the room hoping to be ignored. I had avoided taking this course for a year because I had heard via the grapevine that it was difficult. But I desperately needed to get a good grade to raise my overall average so I could get into a graduate school. At the time I wasn't really sure what I wanted to study in a graduate program, but if it got me a draft deferment that was all I really desired. Little did I realize then that one day I would be standing in front of a class facing students who might have the same fears I once had.

The class was supposed to start at eight o'clock and last for fifty minutes. Everyone sat quietly. When ten minutes had gone by students started whispering to one another, wondering if the course had been cancelled. As someone got up to leave, a short, young man, sitting in front of me and hiding behind a newspaper in front of his face, got up from his chair in the back of the room and moved to the front of the classroom. He looked as if he had gotten dressed quickly that morning with no heed paid to coordinating colors or clothes. He wore torn jeans and sneakers and an old tee shirt under a tweed suit coat with these words printed across the front: "Cognitive Dissonance Rules!"

He took out a marker and wrote in big letters across the board: **You don't know ____**. Here we go again, I thought to myself; you'd think he couldn't fool me twice.

He waited for a moment and then asked in a clear, loud voice: "Okay, boys and girls, fill in the blanks. What is it you don't know?"

No one spoke, but there were a few giggles. "Come on, my young Sophists, what's the missing word in this sentence? What it is you don't know?" Still no one raised his or her hand. The teacher then wrote the missing letters across the board—DIDDLE. There were more giggles and shifting in our seats.

"You may think you know who said this—another dead white man whose picture can be found on the great wall of dead philosophers which hangs in most halls of many college buildings. But I have a surprise for you. One of my students who grew up on the wrong side of the railroad tracks in an urban center once told me the greatest wisdom he ever got came from his mother when he was in his teens and thought he knew everything and said so to his mother. She replied in words that he says saved him more than once: 'You don't know diddle.'" And so I always say: "Mama says: 'You don't know diddle.'

"And that is the truth. None of us knows diddle. We think we do. We pretend we do. But when you come right down to it we are sitting on the vast beach of life looking at a grain of sand while all around us is the great ocean of truth.

"I don't know diddle either. Then, why am I teaching you about something I know nothing about? Because, my little skeptics, I want you to know what I know for cer-

What Is Wisdom?

tain: Nothing. Actually, everything I think I know could easily fit on the message you find in a fortune cookie, and what you find in that cookie may have more wisdom than I have.

The professor moved closer to us. "Okay, take out a piece of paper and complete this sentence: *I was put on earth to_____*. Write down why you think you are there. Don't think about it. Just write down what comes into your mind. Don't worry--I won't grade this. Only you will grade this and only after you lived more than few decades. Anyone care to share what they have written?" No one responded. "I thought not. Because whatever you wrote down is diddle. So what I want you do now is roll your paper into a ball and toss it into the trash can as I bring it around. I will ask you the same question as we end our time together. Perhaps by then you may be able to complete the sentence with some clarity. And this simple activity will be the beginning of wisdom, which has been summed up for everyone in the advice given by the Oracle of Delphi in ancient Greece: 'Know thyself.'

"The more we think we know, the less we really know. That is why, boys and girls, when the Oracle of Delphi told the Greek philosopher Socrates that he was the wisest man alive, he couldn't believe it. He had been going around asking a lot of questions and not giving many answers because he said he was on a search for truth and knew so little—which is precisely why the Oracle called him the wisest of all persons because at least he knew what he didn't know, and this was most important. Of course, asking questions can be dangerous, especially when faced with people who are absolutely certain they know what is true. Socrates was a gadfly, an insect pestering the know-it-alls with questions they couldn't answer. For these questions, Socrates was accused of questioning the gods of his day and poisoning the minds of young people. He was tried and found guilty and forced to drink hemlock.

"Socrates knew diddle, but it was more like manure that would yield better crops. And so I hope it will be for you, too. By the time we spend our required thirty-five hours together in this dismal, cramped classroom, I hope you will realize you don't know diddle either. That, boys and girls, may well be the last time you will have the chance to really be free of all the things other people tell you are true."

"Professor," came from a young student sitting up front. "What did Socrates know? He must have known something?"

"Don't call me professor. Just Plotimus will do. But a good question because the paradox is that while Socrates appeared to know nothing, he really knew something—that when compared with what there was to understand, he knew little if not nothing. He may have claimed to know nothing, but I think we can learn some important lessons about how to live from him. We can learn to be humble about what we claim to know and willing to listen to different points of view. We can learn to listen to others and to admit what we don't know. And we can learn that philosophy is not just about how we think but equally how well we live.

"Okay, out of your chairs and follow me!" Plotimus was at the back of the room as the rest of us grabbed our bags and books and followed. He was heading toward the river, which ran a block from the campus; he waved his hands and continued talking. "This is what Aristotle

What Is Wisdom?

used to do with his students—walk and talk. He was part of what we now call a peripatetic school, thinkers who walked and talked. And why not walk while you think? It gets the blood running to your brain and at least keeps you alert.

"It's what the first philosophers did a lot of—walking and talking. Sitting in rows of chairs facing a learned professor was not how they learned. So we are following their game plan." He stood in the middle of the street, stopping approaching cars, and motioning us to continue walking toward the river. "Behold, another of life's great lessons that some of you learned in kindergarten—Stop, look and listen before crossing any street. If you can stop, look and listen every day, even when you are not crossing a street, you will have spent your time wisely.

His pace quickened as we struggled to tag along. "'So, what is wisdom? It's not opinions because they are easily spoken and just as easily lost. And it's not knowledge either, though that is the great lie fed to you frequently so you will pay your tuition. You can have a lot of book knowledge and still not be wise. So what is wisdom? Does anyone know?" No one spoke but we had reached the river and had stopped walking.

"Gather round, boys and girls, gather round. Stop, look and listen. What do you see? What do you hear?" One student said softly that she heard the rustle of leaves in the wind. Another said he saw the river flowing. Another talked about the sound of water rushing below.

Plotimus paused before speaking again. "And that's how we become wise. We open our ears and eyes and even our hearts to really see and hear and feel what is always in front of us—life. That's all we have really, the now, present. The past is gone, the future not yet here.

A Teacher, His Students, and the Great Questions of Life

This is it. This is about as close to heaven as you get, right here, and right now. And, who knows, maybe if you really learn how to observe what's in front of you, you may learn to see if it points to something more.

"Take the river; what can we learn from it?" Plotimus asked. Some students responded.

"We learn that it keeps flowing and never stays in the same place."

"We learn that it's on a journey, from the rain to the ocean and back again."

"We learn that when it hits an obstacle, it finds a way around."

"We learn that it's persistent."

"We learn that it's the source of growth along its banks"

"We learn we can use it but also abuse it."

"We learn that we really don't know diddle about much—not where the river came from or where it's going and who has floated on it or drowned. We only know what we see and hear right now."

Plotimus stopped for what seemed a long time but was really only a few minutes. "And that's where wisdom comes from--experiencing life. It's the consciousness of being a living creature that is the real aim of life. The river doesn't mean anything except we give it meaning. And giving it meaning is the heart of philosophy. We are the meaning makers and life is our teacher. And, like the river, each one of us is on a journey, toward what end we don't know. But this much I do know: if you are open to what is in front of you, your life has a chance to be all it was intended to be, which is what Aristotle called flourishing.

"So here are a few items for your notebooks, what I hope you will remember. Philosophy is the love of wis-

What Is Wisdom?

dom. Philosophy can help you think more clearly and live more deeply. That's it in a nutshell. It's all you really need to understand."

As we walked back to our classroom I realized that Plotimus seemed a wise man. He asked a lot of questions and still more just when you thought he had an answer. Yet he was humble, saying he really didn't know much at all, even as I marveled at the sweep of his knowledge of civilizations past and present. I could also understand why thinking outside the box might be dangerous, just as it was for Socrates long ago.

We arrived back at the classroom as the time for the class was nearly over. Plotimus said he was going to write a few words of wisdom on the board from a great philosopher, Bertrand Russell: "LOVE IS WISE; HATRED IS FOOLISH."

"I want you to write this sentence down and carry it with you. I want you to memorize it. Repeat it over and over to yourself until you can say it without looking at your notes. And, then, I want you to try something more difficult. Try to live this wisdom in your lives. Class is over. Next time we shall try something very rare and quite difficult—learning how to think.""

Three

What Is Thinking?

I HAD TO ADMIT that thanks to Plotimus, my philosophical studies were neither boring nor difficult, but I wondered how long this would be true. Wait until we get to logic, the only part of philosophy I had ever heard about, mainly from students who were terrified of it. "He goes from talking about rivers to syllogisms," one friend who had dropped the course warned me, "and it's worse than algebra. If you can survive this part of the course, you might actually make it the whole way." I was prepared to be terrified.

When I got into the class, our professor had posted the following on the screen in the classroom:

> All men are mortal.
> Socrates is a man.
> Therefore, Socrates is mortal.

"Well, my friendly Sophists, tell me: was Socrates mortal?"

At first no one spoke up. Then one student in the front spoke up. "Yes, he's dead, isn't he?" There was a ripple of nervous laughter. We were waiting for Plotimus to criticize her—but he didn't "Bingo, you're right," he said. "Socrates is dead; therefore he must have been mortal.

Maybe we should have rephrased the sentence." He went to the board and wrote:

> SOCRATES IS DEAD.
> SOCRATES WAS A MORTAL.
> THEREFORE, ALL MEN ARE DEAD.

"Is this true?"

"Of course not," said another student. "We're mortal and we're not dead."

The class laughed again. "So what's the difference between the two statements? Why are the first one true and the second false?"

"Well," said a student, "both premises are true. All men are mortal and Socrates is dead are each true, but one conclusion is true and the other false. If all men are mortal and Socrates is a man, then he must be mortal. But if Socrates is dead and mortal, it doesn't follow that all men are dead because some men are still alive."

"That's excellent. What we just looked at were syllogisms, three part statements to help us clarify what we mean by making any claim. The first statement is called the premise, the second the inference from that premise, and the third the conclusion. Any syllogism can break down in many ways: the premise can be false and therefore the conclusion will not be true or the premise can be true but the conclusions drawn from that faulty. Just because Socrates is dead doesn't mean all the rest of us are.

"A great deal of thinking in this world is faulty. People make all kinds of assumptions that can't be shown to be true, then draw conclusions they think are absolutely true. The truth is that most of our truths are shades of gray. We can't be really sure about anything although the philosopher Descartes thought he had arrived at a truth that could not be doubted: *Cognito ergo sum.* I think, therefore I am. Descartes thought he could not doubt that he was doubting, which created a mess later on when other philosophers argued Descartes had reduced human beings to thinking machines, leaving out emotions and a whole lot of other qualities we share.

"But let me write another sentence on the board and ask if it is true or false." Plotimus wrote these words and put them in a box:

> Everything in this box is false

"So, is this sentence true or false?"

"It's true," said someone.

"But if it's true, then the sentence must be false because it says so," said another student.

"Well, then, it must be false," said someone else.

"Hold on," another person said, "it can't be false, because it if is it must be true, but if it's true it must be false."

"Is it possible that both answers are true—everything in that sentence is both true and false?" A student in the front row spoke up softly.

"Why do we need to believe things are either one thing or another? Instead of thinking about a question must be black or white, why not just gray? Maybe the answer to the question is not an either/or." Our teacher drew a picture on the board:

What Is Thinking?

"Has anyone every seen this symbol before?" Many hands were raised. "Where?" asked the professor. One student pointed to the shirt she was wearing. "It's the ying yang symbol. Pretty cool, huh?"

"But what's it mean?" somebody asked.

The professor stood up. "It means that everything in life is dynamic, with two forces interacting, ying and yang. It means that opposites are complimentary, like hot and cold or male or female, or true and false. You can't know one without the other. And for Taoists, the teachers who used this symbol to explain the nature of things, it was intended to show that this dualism is the heart of the universe. And if you want to understand this, all you need do is open your eyes to what is around you—night and day, winter and spring, hot and cold." The professor sat down.

"But what's this have to do with thinking," asked a student who had been quiet since the class began.

"Ah, good question," Plotimus quickly responded. "It means we are back to the beginning—none of us knows diddle. We state something we believe in and don't understand why others don't. And the root cause is language. A great deal of philosophy lately has been about the words we use and the meanings we give to them. The big words we use—like God or country—often come with many different meanings, often ones that wars are fought over. It's the symbols that really get us into trouble, the words like God that point beyond themselves to some deep meaning. I once had a student say to me when we were talking about symbols that they really weren't that important. At which point I suggested he take the American flag downtown and burn it at a busy intersection and see how people reacted to this symbol.

"But here's all I want you to remember. Thinking is a difficult process; some people never learn to think at all. You need to be clear what you put words to and be willing to talk with others who might not have the same understanding of a word or two. We live in a time when words are cheap and have so many layers it is difficult to know what anyone really means and almost impossible to share the same meanings."

"Then why are we here together if words are so difficult to share and my meaning might not be the same as yours?" one student asked.

"Because that is what philosophy is supposed to be about—seeking the meanings between and within our words and knowing our limitations. This is not discussion here. We are not engaged in a verbal tennis match to see who can defeat the other person with witty words and arguments. We are here to seek one another's meanings and search for common ground. That's what the word dialog means and why we are still students who try to take Socrates seriously and find a precious jewel called truth. In today's world of lies and half truths, this classroom may be the closest thing to a sanctuary left."

Four

How Do We Know Anything?

My professor entered the classroom a few minutes late while the rest of us waited expectedly, never quite sure what he would do. If you expect the unexpected you are seldom surprised. Or, as he often said to us: "Life operates by indirection. Just when you think you have things figured out, you find yourself on another path."

This morning my teacher was dressed in black from head (a baseball cap) to feet (black sneakers with holes in them). He went to the front of the classroom, looked at the ground, and spoke in a low voice from the lectern, a prop he had not used thus far. Pulling out a small black book, he began to read in a monotonous tone: "Dearly beloved, we are gathered here this morning to mourn the loss of a good friend, someone who has stood by us in the past, but who is now gone. Our friend kept us honest by his truthful words, never claiming to be perfect but only as clear as befits a thinking being. I will miss our friend terribly."

The professor wiped his eye with a handkerchief as if crying, but I saw no tears forming. And by what name shall our friend be remembered?" He went to the board and wrote in large letters across its length: REASON. "Yes, my little Sophists, last night reason died, the death of a thousand misguided conclusions. Reason died neglected and forgotten, alone and weary, beaten down by the careless words of preachers and politicians, slain by the incessant seductive claims of commercials praising one product over another without proof."

"And who killed him?" He paused to let the question sink in, and then said in a loud voice: "We did! We killed reason! And we shall not see the likes of reason again." He sat down, his hands covering his face. None of us knew whether or not to say anything, so we just sat there.

Finally after what seemed an eternity but which only was a minute or so, our teacher stood up. "Dramatic, yes?" he smiled. "But the memorial service was not without merit, because we kill reason a hundred times a day in many, many ways. Socrates talked about reason as being one quality that makes up truly human. Think about it for a minute. What's the difference between our species and other species in the animal kingdom of which we are a part? We behave like animals in many ways. There's a stimulus and we respond, just like animals, often without thinking. We are more like animals than we admit. It's called the three F's of behavior to which every animal responds without much thought—food, fighting and another word I won't use here today, but you know which one I mean. But there may be a slight window of opportunity that a human being possesses, whether it's part of his brain structure or upbringing. There may be a slight second or two before a human being reacts to a stimulus in which he or she can decide whether to act or not. In that split second rests what makes us unique—we think before we decide. We use words and symbols to choose, and in that choice rests our salvation or destruction."

How Do We Know Anything?

My teacher went to the board and wrote the following word in big letters so they went across the length. EPISTEMOLOGY. "That's a fancy word which simply means the study of knowledge. Not knowing is the beginning, but sometimes we needed to be clear about what we do know, even if we change our minds later."

He pointed at me. "Ah, Mr. Morgan, what do you know?" I froze. "Come on, Mr. Morgan, what do you really know?"

"Well, you said Socrates didn't know anything, so I can't improve on that, right?" I looked around hoping others might laugh. They weren't.

"No, Mr. Morgan, Socrates knew a lot but he knew what he didn't know. He knew that reason was most important, but he also knew it had limits. In fact, he said one thing he wrestled with was how best to live. He called that ethics. So, what's one thing you think you do know?"

"I don't know, maybe that I am thinking right now."

"Ah, Descartes' *cogito ergo sum*; I think therefore I am! But when is the now you speak of? And how do you know you're not dreaming? You see, Mr. Morgan, if we are just thinking creatures we have imprisoned ourselves in our own brains. We are thinking machines and no more."

"So how do you know you are thinking? What do you base your knowledge on?" He looked at me, waiting for my answer.

"I suppose just because I am here and my mind tells me so," I said without much resolve.

"Let's try a mini-lecture. I don't do lectures, but perhaps it might help a little if I put some of this into perspective.

"There are two great schools of thought about how we know anything at all. One says we know through experience; this is the school of empiricism. The other says we know through our reason; this is the school of rationalism. Philosophers have been debating these two schools for centuries. Rationalists say experience is fluid and contradictory. Two people can be in the same room at the same time and have quite different experiences. Empiricists claim reason is flawed. They say reason can't know anything directly. It's all about interpretations and inferences.

"I take a more direct approach." He went to the board again and wrote these four letters: T E R R. "There, if you understand what these four letters mean, you will have a way to answer the question of how anyone knows anything.

"If you memorize these four letters when anyone asks you or you want to ask them how something is known, you can use them to find out how they make any knowledge claim. Of course, some people are too smart to say what they know either because they don't want to suffer philosophers asking them how they know something or they really don't know anything. Remember how Jesus responded to Pilate when he was asked how he knew anything? He said nothing, which must really have infuriated Pilate.

"Let's state with the first letter. T stands for tradition and some knowledge claims come from long traditions of study. I think of Socrates, for example, and the Greek tradition of claiming how important reason is in reaching conclusions. Truth based on reason has a long tradition starting at least with the early Greek philosophers, so a person making any knowledge claim could simply say it was based on a long process of human explorations.

How Do We Know Anything?

"The second letter stands for experience, probably the one most people would claim as the source of what they know. I know something because my experience has told me it is so would be one way to say it. In a way, this way of knowing plus reason is the method by which science makes claims—based on experiences over time and tested by reason.

"Reason is the third way people make knowledge claims. Using your reason arrives at truth. Mathematics is probably the most logical use of reason to reach some conclusion, such as one plus one equals two. But rationalists also use reason to reach other conclusions, such as the sun rises every morning. However, as the philosopher David Hume wrote, you cannot be absolutely certain the sun will rise every morning. That is a hypothesis which is true but might be changed; for example, what would happen if the sun grew cold and gave off no light? Not likely, at least for a few trillion years.

"Finally, the four way people claim knowledge is revelation. This claim usually comes with some divine inference, such as God told me or the claim was made by a prophet or was in some sacred book. Of course, it's difficult to prove or disprove such claims."

Plotimus paused for a moment to think. "Of course, everything I just explained to you is a lie. I don't know anything, therefore it makes no difference whether it's true or not.

"Here's your assignment before we meet again. In the next few days every time someone tells you what he or she knows or believe, ask how they know it. They may look at you strangely, but persist. Don't let them make a knowledge claim without justifying it. If you do this until we meet again, you will find most people will stop telling you what they think or believe and at least you can have a rest from thinking too much."

The professor paused and then laughed. "Of course, they may also force you to drink poison hemlock because they grow tired of your question, just like Socrates of old. But you will die happy. Well, maybe not happy, but at least before your times." With that he walked out of the room.

Five

Who and What Am I?

I GOT TO CLASS a few minutes late, expecting to find my professor already at the board writing something cryptic to get us going. The rest of the class was there, sitting quietly, expecting who knows what to happen? He'd stood on desktops, taken us for walks by the river, worn strange hats, and sworn—anything he said to fulfill the first mission of all great wisdom teachers—Wake up! So what would it be this time? I looked at the closet at the back of the room thinking it would make a perfect place for him to hide and jump out to scare us.

It was a rule that if a teacher did not show up after ten minutes from the start of a class, we were free to leave. But none of us left when ten minutes past, then fifteen. As we were about to gather our books together to leave, Plotimus appeared, walking slowly to the front of the room. Placing a recorder on the desk, he turned it on and left. This is what we heard:

> *"Good morning boys and girls. I am the brain of Plotimus, which he removed from his body and placed in this little machine. Pay no attention to the man walking out of the classroom. He is only a body without a mind, something that took place after years of asking impossible ques-*

tions until his mind could stand it no more. Your professor's consciousness is now on a New Jersey beach listening to the waves breaking on the shore and sipping a cold drink while thinking of nothing important. But let me ask you this, boys and girls: Are you listening to the real Plotimus now? Or does he reside in this in this little machine? Or is the real professor resting comfortably on the sands of eternity, which everyone knows is on the Jersey coast. Answer my question soon or he will exist in some other dimension and you won't be able to get grades. Of course, if you would rather not get a grade, ignore this. This is all for today, boys and girls. In a minute I will go back to this machine until summoned again. I have it on good advice that the world will end in exactly fifty-five minutes. Have a nice day and don't run down the corridor. Thank you. This has been a message from your professor's brain which now resides in this little machine."

We sat still for a long minute, wondering what to do when our teacher came into the room and called out from the back. "Okay, my young Sophists, you tell me: Am I the real Plotimus or am I a figment of your curious imaginations and the real professor is in the machine?"

No one spoke at first but finally a student in the front row spoke up: "It's just a voice in the machine; you're the real professor."

"Logical, my dear student, but what if I ask you what is the difference between that voice in the machine and this one which is now talking. Who and what am I really? Am I my body, which houses the brain? Or am I my brain

Who and What Am I?

telling my body what to do? Or am I both? Or, for those of you who believe in such things, am I my soul which is neither my body nor my mind but something mysterious and beyond our comprehension?"

"You're probably both," said one student, "because you need both to function." Another student responded: "But maybe you have a soul that is more than either?"

"Nobody believes in souls these days," a student argued. "I do," said a student in the back of the room, "so I think you are a soul who happens to inhabit a body. And when you die leaves it to return to its source, which some people call God."

Plotimus listened carefully before speaking. "Let's think this through, boys and girls. If I am a body, then my brain dies when it does, right? If I am just my brain, which is contained within the body, it dies eventually as well. If I am or have a soul, which no one has seen, how can I know?

"Oh yes, we could say you are one person occupying one body with one brain in one period of history and when you die, that's it. But let me ask a more perplexing question: What's mind? Or, better, what's consciousness?"

"It's your brain," one student responded.

"But your brain is a physical thing. Consciousness is not. If consciousness is the brain, then it would be like saying music is the radio. It's not. So what is consciousness?" Plotimus let the question sink in.

"I remember what Descartes wrote and it makes sense," said a student. "I think, therefore I am."

"Then if that is true, Plotimus responded, "then thought exists separate from a body, or that machine. Then I am pure consciousness." He let out a "whoooooooooooo" sound, extended his arms outward, and pretended to fly. "Look at me, my body is leaving and soon I will be pure consciousness and can sell many books about my wisdom."

"But can consciousness exist without a brain or a body in which the brain inhabits?" someone asked.

Plotimus paused. "That's the big question. That's what separates those who think we are material substances occupying space and time who die when the material does; and those who think we are more than our bodies and that consciousness exists even when our bodies don't."

"So when we die, what happens to our consciousness?" A student who seldom spoke in class raised the question.

"That's another big question. Those who believe consciousness to be housed in our bodies believe that when the body dies, so does our consciousness. There are others who believe that because consciousness is not materialistic but energy, it survives the loss of the body in which it has temporary shelter. Some believe every individual consciousness is self-aware of itself as a distinct energy, and therefore retains its individuality beyond death. There are others who feel every individual consciousness is part of a greater consciousness from which it has come and to which it goes when the body dies."

"But let's back up a minute and go back to what we talked about before—how we know anything," someone remarked. "I mean, it seems to me we have two distinct and somewhat competing world views of whom and what we are. "

"And what are these two world views?" someone spoke out.

"Well, one could be called the materialist view that I am a material object in a world of material objects. I exist in a certain time and place because that is where

Who and What Am I?

my parents were living when I was born. I am a certain racial or ethnic group from birth and a lot of who I am—how I learn and what I am interested in—were shaped by the genes which comprise my heredity. By and large, because of these factors, I really don't have much freedom to choose. And when I die, that's it. My brain and consciousness is gone."

"And the other view?" asked Plotimus.

"For lack of a better term, you could call it the spiritualist view. This view believes we are more than our brains or bodies, but that something in us, call it the soul, is energy, just as we know what we believe to be the real world is not material but energy.

"This energy may have lived before in another person or creature, but it certainly continues beyond the death of the brain and the body because energy cannot be created nor destroyed. Whether that energy survives with our personalities or not, I don't know.

"Perhaps our individual energies simply return to the source of that energy from which they came." The class was silent, thinking about what the student had said, realizing it opened up a whole new series of questions. As we sat quietly, Plotimus tiptoed out of the room but at the last moment left with one question: "So what's really real, my little sophists?"

Six

What's Really Real?

Plotimus began the class by telling us to pick up our books and follow him. We'd gotten accustomed to such trips and had come to call him the Pied Piper of Philosophy. We had no idea where we were going, although when we usually took a walk we went down to the riverside, sometimes spending more than a few minutes just listening to the water.

"Okay, boys and girls," he said as we left, "this time I want you to walk in pairs and don't speak. All I want you to do is follow the rule you learned in kindergarten but one which is the key to all knowledge: 'Stop, look, and listen.'"

This time we headed away from the river and toward the city square, a few blocks from the college. "Remember," our teacher said as he slowed the pace, "your assignment is to stop when I do, then look and listen." Except for the rustling of shoes on the pavement, no one spoke. "Now look and listen," he said; "and what does anyone see or hear? Just call out when you have something to offer." The words tumbled down one after another.

"Traffic . . . Cars honking . . . People carrying briefcases . . . Coffee brewing . . . A rundown house . . . Papers and trash tossed . . . Children running . . . A radio blaring . . .

What's Really Real?

A woman yelling something ... A misty, smoky sky ... A sycamore tree with its roots coming through the sidewalk cracks ... Lots of people ... A language I don't understand ... My heart beating ... People staring at us ..."

Plotimus waved his arms pointing to everything around us. "Is this all real?" he asked. No one spoke. "Let me try the question in a different way, one that the earliest Greek philosophers might have asked: What is really real? Is everything changing or is there some that never changes?"

"Well, obviously some things change," a student replied, now feeling freer to respond. "I mean, for example, we change. But so do the buildings and things around us, perhaps not as quickly as we do, but over time even rocks change their shapes."

Plotimus thought for a moment before responding. "There's a poem by the Irish poet William Butler Yeats I read when I was in college that still resonates with me. It's about a young girl on a beach somewhere who after looking around pleads: Let something remain! That's the same question the earliest Greek and Indian philosophers wrestled with; they were wondering if there was anything beyond what changes."

"And what did they conclude?" another student asked.

"As always when it comes to human beings, they came up with different answers to the question of what remained after change had taken place. Some argued that change was the nature of reality that nothing of substance remained. Others argued that in the midst of change there were eternal realities, things that did not changed. Plato's famous story of the cave was his way of explaining the difference between becoming and being, between things changing and things eternal. In Plato's story, people are chained inside a cave, facing a wall. There is an opening in the cave behind them and outside people and animals walk and their shadows are cast on the walls. The people inside the cave think reality is a play of shadows, but the real reality, what he called Forms or Ideas, was outside."

"That's sounds a little spooky," a student remarked. "Besides, how could you prove there was anything outside the cave?"

"I suppose you could find a way to get outside," a woman responded.

"And that's exactly what happened," Plotimus responded. One brave cave dweller decided to find a way outside and he came into the light of day and saw things as they were, the Forms and Ideas of Plato. These were the true realities and everything on the cave walls simply shadows. Plato was trying to show the situation we find ourselves in—living in the darkness, seeing only the shadows, while the realities outside were the sources of our knowledge."

"Then was he saying that most of us live in the cave and see only the shadows?" someone asked.

"Yes," replied Plotimus. "We live in the shadows. And when someone ventures outside in the light and returns to tell us, we kill him because we think he is lying. That's what happened in Plato's story. Someone did get outside and returned to tell about, and they killed him. Sounds like a familiar story in human history, doesn't it?"

They had been standing in a circle in the middle of the block. "Come on, let's keep walking," our professor said. "So the question is how does Plato know there is another dimension beyond everyday reality? I mean, it's the same question that could be put to modern scientists who talk about there being many universes, not one. They try to offer their thoughts based on mathematical equations and research; but Plato didn't have such resources, so

What's Really Real?

he based his on intuition. We intuit or know that some things are just true. We know, for example, a triangle has three sides or that the sun rises every day. The reason is that the idea of triangle or the sun rising is already in our minds. So learning becomes remembering what we already know and have forgotten."

"That sounds very unscientific," I said.

"Remember that the early Greeks and Indian philosophers did not have the benefits of telescopes or microscopes, but they did have the benefit of observing nature. If I asked you to build a home for me, how would you do it? You'd have to have the idea of what a house is in order to build it. You'd had to have its essential form in your mind; no matter how different each house might be look, it would be a representation of that form you began with." Plotimus stopped before crossing the street.

"Look at it this way, Plato was not doing math with his description; he was telling a story to shine light on what he was thinking. Because I live in this century and have been taught to believe only what I saw with my own eyes or experienced, I had trouble understanding what he was saying until I look a trip some years ago to hunt for my ancestors in Wales. I remember getting up early one morning as the sun was rising. I climbed the hill outside where I was staying and sat under an old oak tree to watch the sun rise. It may have only been a few second or minutes before I became aware of what was around me and what seemed to be greater than what I was seeing. There was something more going on here. I felt as if I were taking a peep into another world, another dimension, and perhaps more real than the one I was now in. I had what the poet Coleridge called cosmic consciousness, a moment when I saw behind the veil which separates this dimension from another. And when I climbed down the hill and told my story to a local, he smiled and said the Welsh have a name for such experiences. He called them thin places, or moments in this time when we are aware of another dimension, perhaps a timeless one. That, boys and girls, is what Plato meant in his story of the cave."

"Sounds odd to me," someone said. "It seems to me we live in this world and it's the only reality we have. And that's what science is all about, isn't it? Don't we observe this world and test our ideas by experimenting with them many times before drawing conclusions, and even then our conclusions are tentative."

"Okay, let's take science as our guide for a moment," our teacher said. "Do you know how weird some of what scientists are saying today about the nature of the universe, about string theories and black holes in space, and an expanding universe that may be the result of a previous universe? A great deal of what scientists are telling us these days about what's really real make Plato look quite tame."

"Why bother to think about these kinds of things if we can never find answers?" a student walking right behind our professor asked.

Plotimus snapped his fingers together. "Ah, that's the question to ask! And my answer is that the beginning of philosophy is wonder, and it's the same today. Wonder feeds our imaginations and makes life interesting. I think we are here so that this universe has someone to pay attention. Without us, the universe would grow weary."

" If you have ever wondered why you were put on earth, maybe I just found an answer for myself: I was put on earth to wonder why I was put on earth." I waited for my teacher's words, but he just turned and smiled.

Seven

How Should We Live?

SOMETHING WAS QUITE DIFFERENT about Plotimus today. He looked like an Ivy League professor, at least what I imagined a Harvard or Yale professor might look. He was wearing a bow tie and a white button top shirt with tan khaki pants and suede shoes. He even was wearing silver rimmed glasses, the kind you think of Ben Franklin having invented. And when we walked up to the front of the room, he plunked a large notebook down on the lectern, looked at his wristwatch and precisely at 8 a.m. began to speak in a somewhat monotonous tone, keeping his eyes on his notes. Almost without thinking, most of us sat with our notebooks open and pens poised to write down what he said. It was first time we had done so.

"Today you are going to get your money's worth—a real lecture by a real professor. I expect you to take notes because you will be quizzed on what I have said, and I want you to remember everything I said." The pens inched toward the page waiting for words to jot down.

"I want to begin a reasoned synopsis of the existential critique of Kantian ethics from a utilitarian point of view, focused more on the writings of John Stuart Mill than Jeremy Bentham and countering their consequentialist points of view with Aristotle's notion of arête and eudaimonia, even perhaps touching on whether or not we live in a post virtuous age given the fundamental relativistic notion that there are no universal values."

Plotimus paused for a moment, took off his glasses and cleaned them with his handkerchief. I watched my classmates winching and grimacing as they tried to follow what he was saying. Our teacher continued to speak in a nasal tone, his eyes glued to the pages in front of him. "Could you repeat what you just said?" One student sheepishly asked this while other students waited. "No," said Plotimus. But I will do something. He went to the board and wrote done one word, *eudaimonia*. "Here is the word you will find on your quiz. Does anyone know what it means?" Of course no one did. "It's from Aristotle. It's often translated as happiness, but actually what he intended to have it mean was flourish. The purpose of life is to flourish, to be all you can be, to reach your full potential. Happiness is a byproduct of doing so. As a human being you are here to flourish, to be all you can be, which for Aristotle meant to live fully in accordance with your essential rational nature.

"Now I know when I say the word happiness you think of having lots of money or status. But that is not what Aristotle thought at all. He said there were three kinds of life: the active, the sensual, and the contemplative. And by far what separates you from the rest of the animal kingdom is your capacity to think, to reason things through, to be contemplative. I'm sure you know enough about the sensual without me explaining it."

Plotimus took his sport coat, bow tie and glasses off and walked from behind the lectern. "Now my little sophists, what have I just said?" A few students spoke up and said he had been talking about being all you could be. "Does no one remember how I started my lecture?"

One student looked at her notes and said it was something about existentialism but confessed she had no idea what it meant.

"The truth is I said nothing that makes any sense when I first started talking. Just a bunch of strange words connected to make them sound important. And here you sat taking down what I said, copying the words as if your lives depended on them. That's not living; it's thinking about living. It's what a great Danish philosopher by the name of Kierkegaard—no, do not write his name down in your notebooks—said that most of us are like school children copying from the teacher's notebook words about how to live. The truth is I can't do your living for you. You have to discover the way yourself.

"So what we talking about today is how best to live and that is called ethics and ethics is simply practical philosophy. So much for thinking philosophy is abstract and removed from life; it is just the opposite. It is about how to live best. It is a way of life not a series of thoughts about life."

Plotimus pulled a chair out and asked us all to rearrange ours so we formed a circle. "Now this feels better. We can see one another. Let's start with a question. Do you think all truths are relative, say, for example, in one culture it may be possible to kill and in another not to kill?"

"Of course," said a shy student softly. "I mean one culture may reward killing an enemy; another not. One people may think it appropriate for the weak and old to go off to die, others to keep people alive as long as possible."

"So, it's all a matter of local customs?" asked Plotimus. "Actually, initially what was what morality was about—customs? But does anyone see a problem with this view?"

No one spoke. "Well, if everything goes as they say and there are no values that cut across time and cultures, then I suppose it's okay to hold slaves in 19th Century America or not to permit women to vote until the early 20th Century? After all, it's just their customs. We may think it wrong today, but we're looking backward. Think about what people will say about us a hundred years from now."

"I'd hate to think about what they will say about us," one student said. "Yea, we have taken our technology and killed more people and plants and animals than any previous century. They'll call us barbarians."

"We're dealing with big issues now," Plotimus responded. "Maybe we need to get down to some more basic ones. How do you decide what to do, how to live?"

"I just go by the seat of my pants," one student responded. "Sometimes I go with my reason, some times with my intuition. Every decision is based on the situation I find myself in."

"Let me see if I got anything from the money and time I put into getting a doctorate," our teacher said. "The test of a good teacher is making things as clear and simple as possible, but not more so. The best way I know to describe ethics is beginning with a simple statement I often hear people use when they describe something they have done well: 'It just seemed right, fit and good.' Those three words—right, fit and good—describe three great ethical traditions in assessing any situation. Is it right or wrong, good or bad, fit or unfit? Are there some clear ethical rules or principles which permit or prohibit an activity? Is the action good or bad for me and everyone else? And does the decision just seem to fit what is needed? These three categories are enough to judge most ethical situations or decisions."

Plotimus went back to the board. "Let me write down two questions that I do want you to write down and keep handy when you face any big decision about your life. They may help you focus a little on your intentions and the consequences of your decision before you make it."

Across the board our professor wrote two questions:
What if everyone did that?
How would you feel if someone did that to you?

"I want you to ask these questions if you have the opportunity to think about what you are doing before you do it. Sometimes you don't have this kind of time; you are literally thrown into a situation which you didn't choose and within which you have no time to think. But let's just suppose you do have time. Ask these two questions before you act. They may help you sort out the best decision."

Someone spoke up. "I was just thinking about a situation I found myself in yesterday. A really good friend asked if I would pass on to her the questions on an exam I was going to take the period before hers because we knew professor always gave the same test to all her classes. I gave her the questions. After all, she was my best friend. But as I think about now, I think I made the wrong decision. I mean if everyone did what I did, everyone would be cheating and the test would be meaningless. And how would I feel if I knew another student had the questions before I did. It would be unfair."

"So here's your assignment for next time. I want you think about what kind of person you want to be and then what kind of values you think are most important to being that kind of person. Let's say you want to be a kind person. Compassion would certainly be one of the values

A Teacher, His Students, and the Great Questions of Life

you would need. So, here's your assignment. For the next day practice being a compassionate person. Make a note to do so; tie a string around your finger—anything to help you remember. Here's the reason: Aristotle said that our virtues and our vices are habits and we can practice the virtues. So if you want to be a virtuous person, practice what you value that will help you and others; and don't let yourself practice vices because you don't have them under control. Now go and do something virtuous."

Eight

Does God Exist?

OUR TEACHER ARRIVED A few minutes early for class today and proceeded to hand out a slip of paper to every student. "Okay, here's our question today: Does God exist? Write down either yes or no on the slip, fold it in half, and return to me." When all the slips were returned, he proceeded to divide them into two piles, one for yes and the other for no. And then he counted each pile.

Plotimus went to the board and in large, bold letters wrote this: God exists: 17. God doesn't exist: 16. "I guess this means God exists." He sat down without saying anything.

"But you can't take a vote on whether God exists or not," one student protested. "Either he exists or he doesn't."

"Interesting. You used the word "he" to describe God. How do you know God is masculine? Maybe God is feminine. Maybe God is not a person at all, but a source of energy. Maybe God is a figment of your imagination, a big daddy or mommy you invent because life is just too much and you too fragile. I often say to students: 'Tell me what kind of God you don't believe in, because I probably don't either.'"

"Okay, turn your slips of paper over. I have another exercise for you. But first let me tell you a true story. A few years ago someone walking on the beach found a bottle bobbing in the water. He rescued it, took the cork out, and inside found a bunch of sheets of paper on which were written questions. After reading them, he realized they were all questions to God. It wasn't until later that he found out that years before, a priest had asked members of his parish to write down their deepest questions for God and put them on the church altar without their names. And on Sundays he would take one or two and try to answer them. How these questions got in the bottle no one knew. But the questions were good ones that came out of the real lives of people and were all the more interesting because they were offered anonymously. So now what I want you to do is write down your question to God, whether you believe in God or not. Write down the question that really concerns you and that you have never asked before."

Students wrote their questions down. Plotimus gathered them together, closed his eyes, and began to read them one at a time.

"Why do bad things happen to good people?"

"Why do you let bad things happen?"

"Why did you let my brother die in a car crash?"

"Do you have a sense of humor?"

"If you exist, why don't you make it more obvious?"

"Why are there so many religions?"

"I don't believe in you. Does that bother you?"

"How do I know you didn't just create everything and then leave?"

"Did you create the universe out of nothing?"

"If you are all good, where did evil come from?"

"Are you one or many?"

"Where were you before you created the universe?"

Does God Exist?

"Okay, boys and girls, I need to consult with the almighty for a few minutes. Take a half hour break and come back and I promise I will have answers to your questions." Our teacher walked out of the classroom and disappeared down the hallway. We looked at one another, laughed, checked the time, and went outside or to the cafeteria.

When our teacher returned, we were very interested in hearing what he had to say. It wasn't often we got God's answers.

"First of all, boys and girls, I have consulted the Almighty, and the Almighty told me your questions were quite good but only you could answer them, that the reason you were created was to raise these questions and respond to them. It's all about wondering why—this is what God told me. However, the Almighty did go to the board and gave me some thoughts to pass along to you.

"First, you need to figure out how you would know God exists, if God does exist. The Almighty put these four letters on the board, explained each, and said I should pass this knowledge on to you. The four letters on the board were: TERR. Each letter represents a different way of responding by those who believe God exists. T stands for tradition; some speak from a long tradition of people who believe God is real. E means experience; some believe they have had a direct experience of the Almighty. R stands for reason; others believe because of the order of nature and the universe, reason requires there to be a God. And the second R implies revelation; there are a few who claim to have had a direct revelation from God to bring to us.

"Second, the Almighty said it was important to be clear about what kind of God you were talking about.

A Teacher, His Students, and the Great Questions of Life

Was God like us or totally different? Was God energy and not personal? Did God get everything started in the beginning, then leave everything to us? Was there more than one God? Is God all powerful, all loving, and all knowing? If so, how do you explain evil? If God was all loving, why not simply eliminate the suffering caused by evil, whether of human or natural doings?" Plotimus paused to take a breath, then sat down.

"Wait a minute," someone said, "that's not fair. All your supposed Almighty God did was raise more questions. God didn't answer our questions at all."

"I know. I felt that way, too, so I asked him why," Plotimus responded, "and all the Almighty gave me was a wise crack: 'that's for me to know and you to find out.'"

"Did you really talk to God?" another student asked.

"I don't really know," our professor replied, "but I suspect that is what was supposed to happen, not really knowing. It just felt like the tables were turned on me. I wanted answers and all I got were more questions. It's quite frustrating really."

The room was quiet for what seemed a very long time. It felt like everyone had settled into their own questions.

"Tell you what, boys and girls," our teacher said, "I think God just needs more time. So I will take your questions and see if God responds to them before we meet again. Class dismissed."

"But we have another half hour to go," said a young woman from the back of the room.

"It is only time. Take a break. Even God supposedly rested on the seven day. The Great Being will respond to your questions soon."

Does God Exist?

We were in our seats a few minutes early for the next class. Since the last one, we had been eagerly wondering what our teacher would do about God's answers to our questions. Did he even believe in God? No one was sure whether he was a theist, atheist, or agnostic, but he sure did get excited when we discussed who or what God was or wasn't. Precisely at the beginning of our class, Plotimus walked in and started speaking even before he got to the front of the room.

"I tend to trust reason, but something quite strange happened last night. I took all your questions and put them on the desk in my office at home. I looked them over a few times and soon realized I had no way to answer them. After all, I am hardly God. So I left the sheets of paper with your questions on my desk, and when I came down in the morning I found the questions with answers neatly placed near my coffee maker. After all, knowing everything, God must have known that the first thing I do when stumbling downstairs is head to the coffee pot. So, here are God's answers to your questions. You can believe God actually responded or my wife was playing a trick on me or one of our cats decided to have fun. Here are your questions and the answers.

"Why do bad things happen to good people?"

Because the universe is still evolving and so are you. Most of life's suffering you cause anyway. There's a lot of messiness in the universe and you are part of it.

"Why do you let bad things happen?"

Because that's the way I intended it to be. Listen, the big bang wasn't so tidy. Bad things happened then and they still are happening. One of the reasons I created you was to make good things happen, but maybe I made a mistake.

"Why did you let my brother die in a car crash?"

I wasn't driving the car and if I intervened in every near crash I wouldn't be able to do much else and you wouldn't learn to take responsibility for your own actions.

"Do you have a sense of humor?"

I created you, didn't I?

"If you exist, why don't you make it more obvious?"

I like to play hide and seek. It's the seeking that brings you close to me, not the finding.

"Why are there so many religions?"

Because every person and culture sees in me what they want or need. That's not a bad thing, though I am getting more and more upset when some of your religions feed the killing frenzy with wars.

"I don't believe in you. Does that bother you?"

Not at all. Some of my best friends don't believe in me. I'd rather have an honest doubter any day than a pious know-it-all believer. Quite frankly, I am a little tired of people telling me who I am.

"How do I know you didn't just create everything and then leave?"

Yes and no. I did create and then leave for a while, but from time to time I find it necessary to intervene and leave a few hints about how you should be treating one another.

"Are you a man, woman, or what?"

I am the Great Becoming.

"If you exist, where do I find you?"

Look within first, then at nature, then at others. And be quiet.

"Is there a heaven and hell?"

There is no time. Heaven and hell are your inventions.

Does God Exist?

"Are you one or many?"

Both. I am one for those who cannot handle more. I am many for those who see the need for more, but usually I am no more than twelve.

"Where were you before you created the universe?"

Taking an introductory course in theology. No, strike that. Make it an introductory course in philosophy so I could figure out how to respond to questions like yours.

Our teacher smiled, picked up his briefcase and walked out of the room, leaving us to talk about God.

Nine

What Is the Meaning of My Life?

OUR TEACHER SEEMED IN a good mood today as he literally skipped into the classroom at the precise moment it was to start and began to point his finger at each one of us, asking the same question: Who are you? When we stumbled with our responses, he tried to a different question: Point to where you are? Some of us pointed to our brains, some to our stomachs, and a few to more delicate areas, which got some smirking. Growing frustrated at our lack of responses, he tried one last question: Where is your textbook?

Most of us held up the expensive, lengthy text that seemed written to confuse us but still cost more money than we had.

Plotimus stood on his desk and taking the textbook in hand, tossed it in the trashcan behind him. "This is what I think of this book. It's stuffy and pompous and costs too much to boot. Had I read this as my first philosophy text, I would have left the room screaming. I make you a solemn vow—I am leaving the textbook in this trashcan and will never use it again in a class. It is downright unethical to charge that amount to students who struggle to make ends meet. I am embarrassed that I gave in to my department chair who requires every teacher of philosophy here to use the same text. It's a way textbook publishers

What Is the Meaning of My Life?

make money because authors don't get a fair share. And the worse thing is that every year or so they add a few sentences or reading, pretend it is a new version of the text, and raise the price. What a racket!

"Why don't you write your own text then?" a student asked.

"I am. And it won't cost big bucks and be measured successful by how much it weighs." Plotimus jumped down from the desk.

"I'm surprised you don't remember what I said our first day: You are the textbook and you write the chapters over time. It is your book of life. What happens here in this classroom is not real life; it is a chance for you reflect on your own. A paper textbook or video presentation is just extra. What happens in your life is primary. So let me ask another question: What is the meaning of your life?"

Usually we had learned by now to speak out and frequently. But no one responded to the question this time.

"Okay, sorry, but I feel a lecture coming on. Don't take notes. Just listen and then we will talk." He sat down and opened a faded notebook in which we supposed he kept lectures or notes to himself. He coughed, pushed his glasses up his nose, and began to speak.

"The first thing to note is that there are many primary motivations for living, not just to find the meaning of your life, although there are some philosophers who think human beings can be described as being the meaning makers. Others think pleasure or pain is the primary reason for human choices—we seek pleasure and try to avoid pain. Of course, some heady philosophers said intellectual pleasure is the highest and bodily the lowest, but that is what you might expect for someone stuck in their head.

A Teacher, His Students, and the Great Questions of Life

"There are still others who say survival is the meaning of everything. The meaning of life is quite simple: Live or die. Everything else is secondary. Other thinkers say our meaning comes from the will to live or the need for freedom or power. One philosopher has offered a different take that we live to have the experience of being fully alive. If that's the case, many of us are already dead.

"Let me pause and ask you a question: Where do you find meaning in your life? Just call out your answers." Plotimus began to write what students said on the board.

Family.
Friends.
Religion.
Job.
Children.
Music.
Education.

When there were no more additions, our teacher asked a different question. "So where do you think I find meaning in life?" Most of the students said he found most meaning in teaching and learning, some in his family and friends. "Remember what Nietzsche, the philosopher wrote: 'He who has a why to live can bear almost any how.'

But as I get older and know less, I am beginning to feel that the meaning of my life is wrapped up in others. I cannot feel my life has worth all by itself. It's in the connections with others, whether family or friends or co-workers, that my life has meaning. Unfortunately, the culture in which we live talks a great deal about self-fulfillment and esteem and not so much about life with and for others. I always remember a story told by Viktor Frankl, a psychiatrist who survived the Nazi concentra-

What Is the Meaning of My Life?

tion camps. He was asked to explain the meaning of his life, and he wrote it on a sheet of paper, and then asked his students to guess what he had written. One student said: 'The meaning of your life is to help others find the meaning of theirs.' Frankl was surprised because this was precisely what he had written down."[1]

"Aristotle once said there were three basic ways people found meaning in their lives," our professor continued. "One way was the life of pleasure. What brings us pleasure is good; what brings pain, not so good. Of course, Aristotle opted for the life of the mind as the highest good. A second way was the life of action, of being involved in the world. And the third was the life of contemplation, of living a thoughtful life. Of course you can guess which one he thought was most important--the contemplative life, of course. Aristotle even conceived of God as thinking about thought. Now only a philosopher could come up with such a deity.

"But I want to suggest there is more than one way to find meaning in your life. For some, life is meaningless, so the best you can do is live day by day and take out of each day what you can. It's the old 'carpe diem' approach, or 'seize the day.' But I have come to the conclusion that if a person is truly awake to being alive the only real meaning is to be found in truly finding joy in the experience of being alive. It's a way of life, this being aware of being alive. And it takes a great deal of personal discipline to stay awake, something the Buddha taught us."

For what seemed more than a moment, the classroom was quiet, until finally a student spoke up: "But how do we stay awake?"

---

1. Viktor E. Frankl, *Man's Search for Meaning* (Boston: Beacon Press, 2006), 164–65.

A Teacher, His Students, and the Great Questions of Life

"Ah, a great question, maybe the most important question anyone can ask. And my response is not meant to be flippant: You have to stop thinking and practice being awake. The world is full of distractions. Institutions try to make you fall asleep so they can control you. And even you try to fall asleep because it seems so much easier. But to be fully awake you have to practice wakefulness, getting your ego out of the way, taking pleasure in the world around you and accepting whatever comes. And this takes a lifetime of practice." Our teacher stopped talking and sat down. The room again was filled with silence.

Plotimus stayed in the silence with us, but obviously could not contain himself for very long. Being silent is not one of his favorite things. "So, here's the thing—what if there is no final meaning? What if the only meaning is what we make? What if what it really means to be a human being is to make meaning?"

He was now waving his arms in the air, excited by his own words. "What I mean to say, boys and girls, is that the only meaning is what you make. There is no great plan, no God or gods, no heaven or hell, no religion with all the answers. I know, I know . . . you desperately want to believe that everything has a purpose. You have to believe this or all of life's incompleteness and suffering means nothing. Life is full of sound and fury and means nothing, as Shakespeare put it. You come from nothing, burst into this world without a word or thought, spend your life trying to figure out what it means, and then die and disappear. How's that for a way to live?"

"But you can't possibly believe that," says one student. "No one could live that way without going crazy."

"Ah, but you are wrong," our teacher responds. "'This is it, boys and girls. Right now is all you really have and

What Is the Meaning of My Life?

it, too, will disappear in the blink of any eye. What you think you know doesn't last, and you don't either; then life takes on a new meaning. You learn to value the time you have because it is really all you have. And that's the meaning of life."

He picked up his books, smiled, and left the room. "Well, that's a real downer," someone said as we left the classroom.

Ten

What Is the Meaning of My Death?

"This will be the shortest class on record, boys and girls. I have only one question for you today: Do you believe you will die?" Our teacher folded his arms against his chest and stared out at us. No one responded.

"Ah, I thought so. None of you believe you will die. Being young, you think you will live forever. Well I've got news for you. You won't. Go think about that. Class dismissed." Plotimus grabbed his backpack and walked out of class.

The next class period our professor walked in and while on the way up front asked: "Well? Have you thought about my question? Do you really believe you will die? What have you decided? Let's take a vote. All those who think they will die, raise your hands" All hands went up. "Aha, I thought so; you know you will die because every one of you knows you have to die, but let me ask the question in a different way: How do you feel knowing you will die?"

There still were no responses; so our teacher launched into one of his impromptu speeches.

"Then I will speak for you. You have again shown that the human species avoids the thought of death like no other thought. Underneath this denial are feelings of anxiety, fear, and hopelessness because each of you re-

What Is the Meaning of My Death?

ally feels you cannot avoid death so why think about it? So while you may stop thinking you cannot stop feeling and these feelings are the hard ones to deal with. But they do not disappear, go poof in the night like bad dreams. These feelings stay with you and without much thought you work them out in unthinking ways—racing faster and faster to avoid them until one day the feelings boil over and erupt in conflicts, whether within families or between nations."

Plotimus went to the blackboard and wrote these two words: PASCAL'S WAGER. "Here are two words that create more problems for people than any I can imagine. The philosopher Pascal used them to convince people to believe in God. He basically asked you to take a wager and bet on God, for what would you have to lose? If there is no God and no immortality, then you wouldn't know. And if there was a God and you bet on this God, you might get eternity. Not a bad gamble, you might argue. But what a farce! What kind of God wants you to believe this way, a kind of trick? And what kind of person lies to win eternity, wagers all on a fabrication?

"So burn me at the stake or fire me, but I want to offer you a clear sighted, honest alternative. What if I just tell you there's no God and no life after death? How would that change how you live now, boys and girls? Come on, speak up!" He folded his arms, stared at us, and waited. Still no one spoke.

"What if there is no God and no life after this one? How should you live now, knowing this?"

A student in the front row spoke softly: "I believe in God and I think people will live after they die, and I've never honestly thought about the opposing view, so it feels strange asking it."

"But if this were it, if there was nothing beyond this life, I might live differently," said another student.

"Aha, that's what I want you to think about," said our professor. "How would you live in a world without God or your own immortality?"

"Well, for one thing, I wouldn't worry so much about tomorrow. Today is probably the only thing I really have, and even here I may not have that." The student paused before concluding. "And if today is all I have, I guess I would want to live as much as I could today."

"And that would mean you'd go out having fun and not taking anything seriously," another student commented. "Why bother to plan for the future if there is none or even do good deeds when it doesn't matter anyway because nothing lasts."

"Okay, take out a sheet of paper," said the professor. "I want you to make a to-do list, only make it for this day only. Think what you want to do if you knew for certain your life would end at midnight and there would be nothing beyond that. Okay, think and write."

Our teacher sat down and waited.

After what seemed a long time but was closer to ten minutes no one had yet spoken up. "Okay, boys and girls, still no thoughts? Here's what I want you to do. Everyone up and move your desk out of the way and get on your backs on the floor. Come on, everyone, move!" We did, hoping no one walked by the classroom and looked in.

"Okay, no talking. Stop breathing, too. No, just kidding. I officially declare each one of you dead. Now you are a ghost, staring down at yourself. Complete the following statement for yourself: Looking back, I wish I had_____. Okay, complete the sen-

What Is the Meaning of My Death?

tence in your mind. What do you regret never having done with your life?"

One student spoke in a quiet voice: "I wish I had taken more time with my family."

Another said: "I wish I had pursued painting. That's what I really enjoyed. Now look at me—I'm a business major." Still another replied: "I wish I had wasted time. No, that's not the right word. I wish I had taken time to take walks."

"Come on, class; there must be more regrets."

"Maybe I regret smoking because I remember my sister dying from lung cancer," said someone. "And I wish I had texted less and listened more," said a young woman.

"Okay, everybody sit up. No, stand up. Here's the good news. You are alive. You don't have to live with regrets. You can change. And that's what facing your death means—that you are still alive and can make choices. You don't have to die with regrets. You still have time to live."

"And what have you learned from death?" a student asked our professor.

"The best is to live well, so that when it comes time to die, as Thoreau said, I won't find I had never lived. Or, better, as Mark Twain wrote that when he was dead, he hoped even the funeral director felt bad.

Plotimus went to the board. "Here is everything I think is important in three words." He wrote them in large letters:

LIVE. LOVE. LEARN.

Eleven

Is There Anything Beyond This Life?

PLOTIMUS CAME TO CLASS today, stretched out on top of the front desk and lay there quietly. We waited for what seemed a very long time, until one of the other students stood up and read a note from our teacher. "Dear boys and girls, the shell you see in front of you used to be your teacher. He no longer occupies his body. But where has he gone? Or has he simply evaporated? Go ahead—ask yourselves the question for the day: Is there anything beyond this life? I may or may not hear your responses. But ask away!"

The student sat down. The rest of us felt uncomfortable with a professor up front stretched out on a table. "I think the professor is in heaven, which is where I hope to be one day when I die; so my death is not the end," one student said.

"Who wants to live forever?" Another student spoke out. "I mean eternity seems awfully long. Death is just part of what it means to be a human being and when a life ends that's it. It just ends."

"But that assumes everyone lives to a ripe, old age. What happens if a child dies? Does that make any sense?" A woman who seldom spoke in class looked around.

Is There Anything Beyond This Life?

"Look, my sister died when she was just four years old. Does that make any sense?"

"It's not the quantity, it's the quality," a student responded.

I don't believe that junk!" The woman whose sister had died spoke loudly. "Tell that to my sister who never got to experience more than four years of a life."

"Here's what I think," said a student in the back row. "We live, we die, and that's it, whether four years or eighty. So the meaning of my death is to live as well as I can while I still am alive—it's that simple."

As we grew quiet one student went up front and turned the projector on. "Our teacher asked me to put this up for us to think about after we were done arguing."

The words on the screen began with a question and ended with five statements.

What happens to you after you die?

Nothing.

Something continues, whatever you want to call it—spirit, personality, soul.

You become part of a greater consciousness and lose your own.

You come back in another form.

Nobody knows.

And then a second question appeared on the screen: *How would you know which answer is the right one?*

The students looked at Plotimus who was still and quiet, then at one another, then they launched into a discussion.

"Well, it seems to me you won't know until you die."

"But if you're dead and your consciousness is gone, how would you know anything?"

"Someone would have had to die and come back."

"Jesus did."

"Well, some people think that's a story people made up after he died."

"What about people who have been declared brain dead, then come back to describe being someone else and not wanting to return?"

"I've read about this but I've also read some scientists say that when death is near, the brain releases chemicals that give you a high and can create all these illusions."

"Maybe our individual consciousness doesn't survive intact; maybe it just becomes part of some greater energy."

"How would you know this if you lose your personal identity?"

"Maybe our energy comes back and takes a different form; you know, reincarnation."

"Does anyone here really know they lived before in some other form and can tell us about it? And if we don't remember who or what we were before, how can you prove it?"

"Why do we need to think we will live forever? Why can't we just enjoy life now and when it ends, accept the fact we are gone?"

"Because deep inside each one of us is afraid. We cling to life and don't want to face its extinction."

"But then life isn't fair. Some people get a full life, others very little. Some have rough lives, some easy ones—and just because they were born into the right or wrong family at the right or wrong time. It seems so unfair."

"I think I remember from our readings that one philosopher had to postulate immortality for this reason. Without it, life seems cruel."

Is There Anything Beyond This Life?

"Whoever said life was fair? Why not just say it's all a crap shoot, live well while we are conscious, and then let go?"

"Didn't that guy we read early on, Socrates I think, say when facing his own death that he wasn't afraid? I think he said that if there was nothing beyond this life, he wasn't afraid because it would be like a good night's sleep. And if there was something, he looked forward to seeing his friends and family again."

"Seem very rational to me."

"But that's the problem. Our fears are not rational. Something else in us cannot face our own extinction and yearns for more life beyond this one."

Again there was a long period of silence.

"So, what do we do now? The professor is either asleep or fooling us again and we still have a lot of time left before we have to leave. Does anyone have anything to add?"

"I remember our teacher telling us once that the principle of the Tao was spontaneity, that life was a game to be played. Maybe we should make up a game about death."

""What do you suggest?"

"Let's pretend the professor has really died and we are at his funeral. What would we say then?"

"I'd say I hope he graded our finals before he died."

"I think he would have planned his own funeral and just as the music started he would pop out of the coffin."

At this precise moment, the professor sat up, looked around, and stood straight standing atop the desk. "Yes, you finally got it right! I was waiting for one of you to say something like this. So now that I have been to the other side, I have returned to answer your questions about what happens after death. Anyone want to start?"

"Well, okay, let's play the game. Where were you?" The student had a smirk on his face, something he probably learned from Plotimus.

"I don't remember actually. But the feeling was that I was in a safe, warm place, just like I was in my mother's womb before I entered this world."

"So you remember the feelings but no details?"

"Exactly," our teacher said as he stretched. "And now I am ready to return." With that he placed his arms out front like a swimmer about to dive into the water, and jumped. "Back to this dimension, having been to the other," he laughed.

"But where were you?" asked someone.

"That's for me not to remember and for you to guess. That's the final exam each one of us has to take. What did you do with your short time on earth and in this dimension? And how you answer that will shape where you end. It's all in the mind anyway."

"So there's nothing beyond this life?"

"I didn't say that. I just don't know. I could ask different questions and get different answers. Where was I before I was born? Is it any more astounding to believe I was somewhere before I was born than that I become someone after I die? "

"This is a joke," said another student. "What kind of game is this when someone pretends to come back from the dead and has nothing to tell us about where he was?"

"Each one of us enters life with a cry and getting slapped. If anyone has a memory of where they were before birth, they don't say. Each of leaves the planet without telling others where they have been. But at least you don't get slapped on departing--which is about what I am now about to do.

Is There Anything Beyond This Life?

"I have one last assignment for you to complete. Take out a piece of paper and complete this sentence: *I was put on earth to* _____." Our teacher waited for us to complete the exercise, then advised us to fold the paper up and keep somewhere we could look at from time to time. Plotimus waved goodbye and left the room. I didn't see him again for a few months when I think I saw him leading a class down by the river, waving his arms and pointing to the sky above and then the earth below.

Twelve

What Is Time?

OUR TEACHER WOULD OFTEN suggest that philosophy is not so much about concepts or even philosophers, but more about stories. He called it "narrative philosophy."

I remember one of the first classes I took with him that he had us hold up our textbooks and then he took his and threw it in a wastepaper can. "This is what I think of this text, which costs more than you can afford and is full of a few introductory comments and then the writings of philosophers. I don't object to you reading philosophers, but I do resist others putting their words together in a book and calling it worthwhile."

He would then explain philosophy as a collection of stories, many of them organized around the questions of life. "You are the textbook in this class," he would explain, "and you are writing the chapters of your life even as we meet. Roughly speaking, every seven years equals a chapter of your life; some of you have three chapters done already, some less, and others more. And while you are not completely in control of the plot, you have some power over the narrative. You can make choices, you can turn your life around, and this is what philosophy is about—making choices, having some power over your

What Is Time?

own life so that you do not end up at the end at the chapter wondering what it was all about."

Our professor would then ask us to develop our own book of life, breaking each chapter down into about seven years. Most of us were either beginning or into our third chapter. And once our book was done, he would ask us to share it with others in a small group because he said that is where philosophy happens, in dialog with one another. And then when we had shared our story, he would ask us to think about when we might die, picking any time of our life, and reflecting on the previous chapters. Philosophy, he would say, is about understanding our lives, reflecting on them, and coming to terms with one's self.

And then he would ask: And what time is it now? And each of us would check the clock on the wall or our own watches or cell phones and he would laugh. "No, not that kind of time. I want you to think about time itself. What is time?"

And when we had discussed the question, he would tell us that time itself is an illusion, although it feels very real, and the only way to measure it was by telling our stories or inventing them to point to the passage of the hours and days as if time were real. Our assignment then became to write a story about time to share with children. Plotimus required each of his students to read a story to children in a nearby school. "It's the only way you will learn what philosophy is," he would say. And each of us would struggle writing a story and later tell it (he would not permit us to read the story in the classroom but rather tell it).

Looking back now I know that he was right—our lives are stories and we write the chapters over time with the help of others. Some of our stories are sad, some funny;

but all are interesting. Everyone has a story, but few of us listen, even to our own tales. It was our teacher's way of reminding us of the wisdom of the oracle of Delphi in ancient Greece: "Know thyself."

Our final assignment was for the entire class to write one story to respond to the question: What is time? If you think writing such a story for children is easy, try it. It required us to tell stories, argue about them, but finally under the pressure of the end of a class, end. What follows here is the story of a small boy, old man, and a dog—written to help children wonder about time.

Story of an Old Man, A Boy, and His Dog

(1)

The boy tripped over the old man's foot, which was sticking out from a homemade hut by the riverside. The boy was startled, thinking it was another body found by the river where so many others had been found, the results of drugs or sub zero weather. But it was spring, and by all rights a season of rebirth, not dying. But a foot it was, and was soon followed by a grunt, then words the boy could not make out. He froze and watched as an old man emerged from the fragile structure. The man was older than anyone the boy could ever remember seeing. The man's hair and beard were snowy white, overgrown and matted with leaves.

The boy had wandered off the trail where he took his dog for a walk each morning before school. He had seldom encountered anyone else walking here so early in

What Is Time?

the morning because they had heard stories of its strange inhabitants, many living under the bridge. But they usually left before dawn. But the boy had gotten up early so he could return home before breakfast to write a short story for his fourth grade class at Keystone Elementary School. He was known for his stories by the other students, and since he couldn't kick a ball on the soccer field or hit a shot on the basketball court, writing stories that could be shared in class was his chief way to be noticed at all, having come to this new large school in the fall from a nearby small village.

The old man stopped and stared at him, and noticed the dog. "What's his name?" "It's a girl," the boy responded, "and her name is Sophie." The old man stretched, then bent down and held out his hand to pet the dog.

"Sorry I woke you up," said the boy. "I just didn't see your foot."

The old man was quiet for a minute. "Well, no wonder. It surprises me that I am here, too. I fell asleep last night while on a trip and must have landed here?" He stretched. Answer this please: "Where is *here* anyway?"

"Where is here," the boy questioned? "Here is right now where it's always been."

"But where is the now that I just missed?" The old man chuckled, then sang a song: "If now is past and past is gone, then what's here right now is nothing. Since the future isn't here just yet, I have no idea about much of anything." He took a deep breath. "Guess I better work on my song style. It's been a long time since I've sung."

"I don't follow you," said the boy.

"Sometimes I don't even follow myself," responded the old man. "In fact, there are days when I line up behind myself and still get lost."

A Teacher, His Students, and the Great Questions of Life

"Say, who or what are you and why are you here anyway?" the boy asked, suddenly thinking he might find a good story for his class today.

"It's a long story," the man responded . . . "I suppose like everyone else you don't have time for stories. Probably like everyone else you're racing around like a bat out of hell. That is, if you believe in hell."

"You're right, I am in a kind of rush" the boy replied. "I've got to get going to school. But I love stories. I've even written a few. When I grow up I want to write stories to make people laugh or cry but mainly just to get their attention." Something in the look of disappointment on the old man's face made the boy add: "But I could come back here after school and listen to your story. Would that be okay with you?"

"If you want to come back after school today, I'll be here."

"I'm supposed to write a story for my class about someone I've met, you know, the most unforgettable character type of story. Can I write the story about you since you're the first person I've ever met sleeping by the river?"

"Ah, the holy river, you mean? For it is holy. Everything you need for your story about me you can find by sitting quietly and listening to the river; she does speak, even before your kind was not on earth. The river tells everything you need to know—about time itself. It stops for no one. Did you know you can't step in the same river twice because it changes before you can? How about this one: the river comes from the sky and the streams and the lakes and returns to the ocean from which it starts all over again. It's all there and my story is part of the river's story." The old man was quiet and the boy listened

What Is Time?

to the river and for a minute imagined he could hear it speaking.

"If you bring me a sandwich and a bottle of water, I will tell you my story," the old man said, as the boy and his dog walked away. The boy waved goodbye and nodding he would return.

The boy sat through another boring school day; most of the time he was thinking about the old man by the river. How did he get there and what did he do all day by himself and who was he and why was he there? The questions kept on but the boy realized he had no answers. He wished time would go by more quickly, but the minutes dragged on for what seemed a very long time. Time? What was it about time, the boy thought, that when you think about it seems to go slow but when you forget it speeds up? He laughed to himself—the old man must have gotten into my head.

The boy thought a lot about time lately since his father died a month ago. He hadn't been there when it happened. One day he had come home from school to find his mother crying and his father gone. She explained that his father had had a heart attack and was gone. "Where did he go?" the boy asked. His mother had responded: "to be with God." The boy was angry with God for taking him. Instead of saying a blessing before meals or a bedtime prayer as his mother had taught him, he retreated into silence and stayed there even when he was awake. When teachers would call on him in class, he would simply say he didn't know the answers, so eventually the other children thought he was dumb and the teachers that he was a slow learner. They had sent him to the school counselor who asked a few questions and sent him back to classes with a word or two about taking time to get over things.

A Teacher, His Students, and the Great Questions of Life

Everything takes time away from us, he thought to himself, until nothing remains, not even memories. So what good was it to stop thinking about time?

The school bell rang at three o'clock and the boy put his books in his backpack and walked home alone. He came home every day to find an empty house because his mother now worked, but she always left him a note on the kitchen table to remind him to do his homework or finish a few chores. Today the note was brief: "See you at dinner. Love, Mom." The boy was going to unpack his bag and get his homework done, but he remembered the old man and wanted to hear what he had to say, so he made a sandwich and grabbed a bottle of water and he began to walk as quickly as he could to the river, only a few blocks from his home.

(2)

When the boy got to the place where he had first encountered the old man he found the hut empty. He peeked in. There was no one inside. He thought perhaps the old man had already left until he happened to glance up and saw a pair of legs dangling over a tree branch. He was startled and blurted out: "Hey, what are you doing up there?" The old man looked down. "Waiting for you and watching the river. It's so much nicer up here. Besides, it can change your whole perspective on the world if you just move where you are. So my question is: What are you doing down there?"

"Keeping my feet on the ground," said the boy, "which is what my father used to tell me is most important—that and keeping my nose out of other people's business."

The old man paused, his brow wrinkling from thought. "Yes, good advice, but I think it also helps to keep your

What Is Time?

eyes on the sky above. Maybe the two of them together make the most sense—keep your feet on the ground and your eyes on the heavens." He chuckled.

The boy looked up again. "I don't think I could climb this tree. So how did you get up there?"

"I flew," said the old man.

The boy's shrugged. "You can't fly. And you're too old to climb. So how did you get up there?"

"I told you the truth," said the old man; "I flew."

"So fly down then," the boy challenged, "and I'll believe you."

"That would be easy," the old man responded, "but I think you would learn more if I helped you fly up to where I am."

"Impossible," the boy replied.

"Close your eyes then. And follow my instructions. Are you ready?"

"I suppose so, but I'm not falling for any tricks either."

"Just listen to my words, boy. Close your eyes. Believing is seeing

"I always say, believe you can fly. I mean really believe you can fly. Imagine yourself being lifted off the ground. That's it. See yourself slowly rising toward me. It's as easy flying as walking, just different things your mind can help you do. Your mind is telling you to float up to me. Listen to it."

The boy opened his eyes and was very surprised to find he was sitting beside the old man. "Hey, I am sitting on the branch with you. How'd you do that trick?"

"I didn't do anything; you did." The boy handed the old man the sandwich and bottle of water. The man began to munch on the sandwich and talk. "Your mind is a powerful thing. If you believe that, you can do pretty much anything you want or go anywhere."

"Anywhere," the boy asked?

"Sure, anywhere," the old man responded. "Here, hold on to my hand and I will take you to where I live."

"Where's that?" the boy asked nervously.

"I call it Pantisocracy. It's not a place but a state of mind. Take my hand. I'll show you."

"Wait a minute," the boy said as a dog stared up at where they were sitting. "I can't go without my dog. She'll want to go along."

The old man looked down. "Dogs have minds, too, so why don't we will ourselves down to the ground? What's your dog's name?"

"Sophia," the boy said, "but we call her Sophie." He suddenly noticed all three of them were now standing together on the ground.

"A wise name," the old man laughed. "You probably don't know it yet, but Sophia is Greek and it means wisdom. And the love of wisdom is called philosophy, and that's what we are going to explore together."

"But what should I call you?" asked the boy.

"I have many names but for now just call me Socrates—that's as good as any name. And by what name do you go?"

"Adam," said the young boy.

"Ah, perfect," said the old man. "You will be the first man, I the philosopher, and your dog will be wisdom. We will make a great trio for our adventure. In fact, I am going to help Sophie speak as we do, with words and gestures, though I often think she might be better off without words because she can know things as they are and not as we express them. Here, Sophie, use your mind

What Is Time?

and speak as we do." Sophie wagged her tail and tried to bark. At first the barking was faint but then disappeared until finally a word formed that sounded a mix between growling and speaking. "I . . . can . . . speak . . . as you do!" she exclaimed, running around in circles, panting and wagging her tail. "I can speak! I can speak!" And she laughed so that it sounded like a strange combination of barking and laughing.

Socrates waited for Sophie to stop running in a circle, then asked Adam and Sophie to hold hands and paws. "Now close your eyes. And when you open them we shall be in a new land."

"'Will we be in Pantisocracy?" asked Adam.

"Yes," said Socrates, "it will be. But remember, it's not a place in time. In fact, there is no time here at all. It's what you mortals call 'eternity.'"

"You mean heaven?" Adam asked.

"If that's the best word you know, I guess it is," Socrates replied, "though it's really just another dimension which has always been there in front of you. You just haven't been able to go there until now."

"Will my father be there?" Adam asked quietly.

"If he's where there is no time he will be," replied Socrates.

"Are there more dogs here?" Sophie asked. This really surprised Adam since he had never heard his dog speak before.

"Sophie, you can talk! I can understand you!"

"Well, I've always understood you, Adam, but I never had words before, and I will confess this is quite different for me as well. I think I am still barking but you hear what I mean."

A Teacher, His Students, and the Great Questions of Life

"Words usually get in the way," said Socrates, "but we are communicating with one another in our minds, and therefore what we are thinking is quite clear. This is the way it once was in your world of time. That's one of the things so unique about Pantisocracy. Every living being can understand each other—people and animals and trees and rivers and even the ground upon which we think we now stand."

The next second Adam felt his world disappear. It was like being in a dark tunnel; ahead he thought he could spot the light at its end. He looked to his side and watched what seemed to be a movie; he saw people he thought looked familiar waving to him.

If the others are seeing what I see, they are going to be very surprised, the boy said to himself as he watched stars fly by. It was quite dark at first. He wasn't moving, just watching. In fact, he wasn't sure if he even had a body. No, he was almost sure he didn't have one. But, then, what was he without a body? He thought for a moment he heard Sophie speak, but he couldn't see her. Ahead he imagined he saw a light in the distance. And suddenly he could see a figure standing in the light, waving to him, making gestures with his hand to urge him on. It was Socrates, or at least what the old man called himself, and beside him was Sophie.

"Now you can get back into your body if you wish," said the old man. "Your dog and I have already done so. But first close your eyes and take a few deep breaths before you open them. Sometimes it's difficult for the mind to enter the body again; to the mind, the body seems a prison."

"And I don't mind telling you that having three of you standing on me is no fun," a voice said. It was the earth beneath him speaking. "Sorry," said Adam as he looked down, "we'll step lightly."

"That's better," replied the earth, suddenly recognizing one of them. "Ah, old man, welcome home! I didn't recognize you right away. Who are these creatures with you?"

"These are my friends from the other dimension, Adam and Sophie."

"Well, ask them if they will take off their shoes," the earth said and then chuckled. "Obviously the one creature has no shoes to take off."

The boy took off his shoes. "So this is Pantisocracy?

"Just the road to Pantisocracy which you can see ahead," said Socrates.

Adam looked. There were two roads ahead. One headed into what seemed a grove of trees and the other was lost to sight as it took a sharp turn to the right.

"And which road shall we take?" Adam said turning to Socrates.

"Makes no difference in the long run," said Socrates. "Both roads lead to the same place although the journeys along each may be different. The question is how do you decide which one to take?"

Adam pondered the question. "I suppose if I were really wise I would ask someone who had already been down one road and could tell me what each was like."

"That might be one way," replied Socrates, "but remember though the roads may look alike, everyone discovers something different along the way. It is said that especially wise persons make the road unfold before them; they have such powers."

"The power of the mind again," said Sophie. "Why don't we just take one and find out for ourselves?"

A Teacher, His Students, and the Great Questions of Life

"That's the only way to find anything," said Socrates, as the three walked very softly over the earth and took the road that looked less traveled by.

(3)

The three friends had been walking for quite a while before the boy stopped to take a breath. "What's the matter?" the old man asked. "I'm tired," the boy replied.

They sat down by the side of the road. "We've been on the road a long time and except for trees, we don't seem to be near anything," said the dog.

"Well, aren't we good enough?" a voice barked.

"Who was that?" Adam replied. And then he watched as the branches of a bush bent down. "Are you talking to us?"

"Yes, indeed" came the reply from somewhere inside the bush. "What are we, saw dust or something? We can hear everything you say, you know." Suddenly there were quite a few bushes by the side of the road that Adam hadn't noticed before, and each one's branches were blocking the way forward. "Yea, what's the matter?" all said at once, their voices quite loud now. "We are here just as much as you are."

Sophie was about ready to relieve herself on one of the bushes when she realized that would not be such a good idea, so she ran off out of sight to take care of her needs. "At least you dog shows respect," an old elm said, joining in. "Yea, she knows not to bark up the wrong tree," responded a sycamore as the other tree and all the bushes laughed.

"I really do beg your pardon," said Adam. "I forgot I'm not home any longer."

What Is Time?

The old man spoke. "You'll have to excuse them my leafy friends; this is their first time to Pantisocracy, so they have not yet gotten use to the idea that every living being here has consciousness."

The old elm thought for a moment before saying anything as a bird flew out of its branches. "But that's the prime teaching here—that everything is a part of the whole *and* knows it. Think what might happen if we didn't realize this and went around doing whatever we like to whatever we wanted. Why sooner or later we'd lose sight that we are all connected to one another."

"Yes," said another, tree, the willow, weeping, for willows are known to be exceedingly sensitive. "We'd lose our understanding of the primary rule: Treat others as you would wish to be treated because they are you and you are them.

"The dog and boy have a similar rule where they come from," said Socrates, "but they talk about it a great deal but seldom live by it. In fact, I've often thought they ought to compose a new one: Do unto others before they do unto you. That would closer to how they live."

"My, what a horrible way to live," replied an old oak, considered the wisest among the trees. "Saying you believe one thing and then living just the opposite. That is the worst way I can think of to live. Imagine their poor saplings that hear their parents say one thing and then live another way. It would create a terribly fearful place to grow up. Here at least our roots are deep and our branches reach out to touch one another without fear of being harmed. I can't imagine a world without the primary rule being practiced."

"I'm afraid where I come from they cut trees down and burn them to heat their homes," said Adam softly.

The willow was weeping more now than before. The old man patted the willow's bark gently. "There, there, my compassionate friend. Don't cry. I've brought Adam and Sophie here to learn a different way of life, hoping they might take back our way to their world. Who knows, if they could teach others our primary rule they might even save a few trees if not the whole planet."

Adam looked at the old man. "Is that why you brought us here?"

"Yes," said Socrates. "I have spent enough time on your planet observing how you treat one another and what it has done. My heart has been broken so many times by your sufferings that I could stand it no longer."

"But I am just one boy and Sophie one dog," Adam replied. "How could we make a difference?"

"First things first," the old man responded. "You must follow the path of your choice here to see this world and understand it, so you can take what you have learned and share it with others in your world."

"But we are only two small creatures, and the world is so big and dangerous," said Sophie. "I don't think we can do much."

"Maybe, maybe not," the old man responded, " but I have chosen you both to take the word back to your planet. That's all you can do. They will have to make the choice."

Suddenly the branches were saving back and forth and the trees speaking with one voice. "Yes, you must try. Our primary rule says as much and we are bound by it. We cannot be happy now without helping others. You are connected to us and just don't know it yet. Maybe if you realize this, others on your planet can as well."

What Is Time?

Hearing so many voices with one message, Adam turned to Sophie. "I suppose we must try, Sophie, for unless we do our home will be lost forever."

"But which road do we take?" Sophie asked.

"Listen and watch what the trees say," Socrates replied.

Adam watched the trees as their branches all turned to the east and their voices said quietly like the wind blowing through their leaves: "This one, this one. Take this one."

And so the old man, the boy, and the dog followed the path eastward as the trees applauded, the sound of their branches clapping in the breeze.

"We've been walking for a time," said Adam, as he sat down by the side of the road and Sophie ran off to sniff a bush. "I don't think we are learning anything."

"Ah," Socrates smiled. "Then you are ready to learn. A long time ago on your planet a wise man bearing my name was told he was the wisest of all just because he said he didn't know anything. But he knew quite a lot really, even if it was like a grain of sand on the beach of the universe. So, Adam, tell me what you don't know."

Adam thought. "Well, I don't know where I am or what I am doing here. I don't even know if this is all real or I am dreaming." He pinched himself. "Ouch. I guess at least I am awake."

Sophie came back from her sniffing and lay down on the road. "Seems to me that we need to pay attention to what Socrates said to us in the beginning. Our minds are pretty powerful. If that's the case, we can forget about which road to take and just imagine where we want to go—and then we shall be there."

"But that's the problem, Sophie, because we don't know where we want to go. And if we don't know that we're likely to end up going around in circles, which is what we've been doing." Adam took a deep breath and stood up.

"'Everyone wants to go somewhere," Socrates said, "but when they get lost they run twice as fast to get somewhere, and get even more lost. Sometimes the best you can do is stop running and ask yourself one question: What I am really looking for?"

"I'm fine with the journey," Sophie said. "Dogs sometimes just like to sniff and head in no particular direction."

But when we started out, we were trying to understand where we were and what it means, Adam thought to himself. And then he said: "Actually what I want to find out is what happened to my father and whether he is still alive somewhere."

The old man nodded. "Yes, I think that is a good place to begin. And, if you remember, all of this is in your mind—the trees, the road, even me. This is your reality so you might as well use it. Your father's gone from one dimension but could be in another. Perhaps if we all wished hard enough together, we could go there now because the road is already inside you, Adam."

Adam closed his eyes and tried to remember his father, wishing he could speak with him again.

(4)

When Adam opened his eyes, he found he was alone. He had no idea where the old man and his dog had gone. But he was in a grove of apple trees; he could see them on the trees, some were green and others red. He was hungry,

What Is Time?

but he also remembered the other trees he had encountered, so in a soft voice he spoke out loud: "Good day, apple trees. I am Adam and I am trying to find my father."

It was quiet in the grove at first except for a few birds chirping in the distance. One of the smaller trees finally spoke: "Glad to make your acquaintance, Adam. I am a young tree, probably about your age. What are you doing here?"

"I was looking for my father actually," said Adam, "but I have no idea where to look."

"What does your father look like?" asked the small tree.

"Like me, I guess, only taller," Adam replied. "I'm not quite sure how I ended up here."

"Well something brought you here," said the tree; "perhaps if you just clear your mind and rest under my branches, everything will become clear.

"Here, pick one of my apples and eat it. Perhaps you are just hungry." Adam picked an apple and began to munch on it. "Aren't you upset I took one? I mean it rightly belong to you."

The young tree laughed. "Oh no, our apples are here to be given away. That is why we are here. The true destiny of an apple tree is not an apple; it is making another tree. Our prime directive is to treat others as we would wish to be treated, so when I say you I said to myself that this boy must be lost and hungry and how would I feel if I were in his roots . . . . I mean, shoes.

So I thought to myself that I would probably want a moment to collect my thoughts, even fill my belly. So that's why I gave you my apple."

"It's your prime directive again. I've been told I came here to learn about it and you have shown me how it works by a simple gift of an apple. Thank you, apple tree. I am learning." The boy put his back against the tree and slid down to a sitting position. "I guess sometimes the best thing to do is nothing but find that calm place within yourself where time is not that important and where you can seek an answer." He soon fell asleep.

When Adam woke he was not sure how long he had been asleep, but he found himself in a new place. He was on the beach somewhere. A few yards away he heard the ocean waves break, feeling the spray and smelling its saltiness. It felt familiar like the summers he and his family would go to the coast. Or was it all a trick? Had he created this scene in his mind? After all, Socrates had told him he could use his mind to create anything. He pinched his arm and it hurt. So he must be in his body or at least his mind had created a reality where things could be experienced as if they were real. It felt good to be here no matter if his mind had created it. He sat still and soaked it in, remembering how as a child he had gone with his father and mother to a summer cottage a block from the house. It was a good memory because he had time to play and sometimes just be around his parents.

He fell asleep again. In a dream he remembered his father's face clearly. He was not sure but he thought he was on his back in his crib and his father was looking down at him and smiling. Then he found himself outside on the front lawn of his house, playing catch with his father and finally sitting down to share a drink and just talk. These were the best moments, he thought, when the two of them could sit quietly side by side and just converse about the day or whatever came into their minds. Perhaps this what time was really about—not the clock or the changes but rather the episodes out of one's life, not

What Is Time?

well knit together life a story book, but brief and vibrant memories, moments in time but out of time when something really important seemed to happen. Who knows, perhaps even now was another of those moments in and out of time where its passage seems frozen like some black hole in space.

He opened his eyes again. It was a bright cool April morning, April 2 to be exact, his birthday. He had been born a few minutes past the first of April, his mother telling him she held on so he wouldn't be an April's fool. He had come downstairs before anyone else got up to see if there might be any presents anywhere, but the breakfast table was bare and he couldn't even see any birthday cards. So he had gone outside on the back porch to sit and rock in the old red chair someone told him his grandfather had made. He heard the screen door opening and someone coming outside. Was it his father? Before he could turn around to look, he woke up, a few lines lingering in his mind: Life is millions of time zones.

"Adam, Adam, wake up!" Was that Sophie speaking to me, Adam wondered as he began to open his eyes? Wait a minute; dogs can't speak like that, can they? And then he realized where he was. "Where's Socrates?" was the first thing he could think of to ask. "Down the road somewhere," Sophie replied; "but the question is where have you been? You fell asleep and Socrates said you probably needed to rest. He said he would take a short walk to see what was ahead, but that was awhile ago."

Adam stood up and stretched. "I don't know where I was and it sure feels like it was a long time ago that I fell asleep."

"Funny thing about time," Sophie said. "I never knew what it was when I thinking like a dog; but now that I have words and can think like you do, I only notice its passing, but for the life of me I still can't figure out its duration. You say you think you've been asleep for a long time, but it was only a minute or so ago that the old man went down the road. You really only have been taking a short nap. So what is this time thing all about?"

"Let's ask Socrates," responded Adam, pointing to the figure of the old man coming down the road.

Socrates was out of breath so he sat down and rested. "I hope you don't mind my leaning against you," he said to the tree. "Not at all. Doesn't bother me," responded the tree.

After a minute or so Socrates began to speak. "Whew, that road ahead looks straight and narrow, but once you get around the bend it enters a deep and dark forest with a path that seems to climb a steep hill. I could only make it a little way, so I think we might consider a different road. I hope you had a nice nap, Adam."

"Well, it didn't feel like a nap at all; more like a very long sleep. And I think I saw my father's face. And I was just about to see if it was him walking to my house. And besides . . . ." Adam stopped speaking and looked at the old man. "Say, what is going on here? Are you and Sophie really here or am I dreaming again?"

Socrates spoke softly. "Maybe it's time to unravel some of this adventure for you, Adam. I didn't think it was the right time when he started this journey, but now it seems like it is. You've experienced what I want to talk about, so let's see if it makes any sense to you."

The old man waited for a minute before speaking, seeming to gather his thoughts. "Maybe the best way to explain this is with a story, one Father Time told me when I was a young man trying to understand myself and the strange world I was growing up in."

I sat on the ground; Sophie rested her head on my lap.

"Once upon a time, everything was divided into two equal halves. One half was like night, the other like day. One half liked to pull things together, the other take them apart. But here's the important thing: When each half tried to take over the other, they were equally strong so neither could do so. And the result was what we call the universe, a dynamic moving energy of seemingly opposite forces."

"What's this got to do with time?" Sophie asked.

"I'm getting there," Socrates replied. "Father Time..."

"Wait a minute," Adam interrupted, "who or what is this Father Time you mention? You haven't told us."

"Father Time, Mother Time, Universal Time, the All Knowing Time—makes no difference what you call it. It's just the reason we are here or anywhere. Father Time is what happens in the universal flow to make sure that not everything happens at once."

"You're losing me," said Sophie.

"Okay, that's why Father Time told me a story, so I could understand. In his story, he called one half of everything Chronos and the other half Kairos. And he said these were the two great forces behind everything. Chronos was the king of everything happening right now, the obvious, clock time if you want. Chronos ruled the world I lived in. And when he wanted to take things away, whether a tree or a person, he did so. It was what we called death, something that scared most of us ... well, to death. Kairos was the other half of everything, the less obvious in our midst, that which was hidden but still there. You can see why Chronos seemed the stronger energy to us, taking everything away."

"You mean like my father?" Adam asked.

"Yes. Most of our time was spent trying to avoid Chronos, but as you can see, that was impossible. Eventually Chronos took everything away. It was quite disturbing really. No wonder our soothsayers tried to give us all kinds of remedies to avoid Chronos—magic chants and potions, talking about dreams while resting on their office couches, trying to live a certain way so we would never face Chronos. Chronos ruled. And eventually we gave up trying to avoid him until one day we realized that what was real was more than met the eye . . . Something else was going on that we were missing."

"And, and . . . . what was that?" Sophie said, her speech half bark.

"It's going to sound strange, I know, but one of us went off and learned how to overcome Chronos. All she did was sit under an old oak tree and refuse to leave until she saw what might help. And here's the strangest part; sitting there under that tree, she realized that within herself was another powerful entity that could help. She called it Kairos. Its job was to counteract the destructive tendencies of Chronos and create, not destroy. And all she had to do was sit still, focus her attention, and wait for Kairos to come. When she returned to us, she said everyone could do the same. By sitting still and not thinking, everyone could discover Kairos. And so we did."

Adam was quiet for a moment before speaking. "I'm not sure I get all of this, but I think what you are telling us is that what we think is real is not all there is, that there is another dimension or energy in front of us if we

What Is Time?

learn how to see it, and that if we want we can use it to overcome the world around us. Is that right?"

"You've got it," replied Socrates.

"And if I do, then it means that I can create a different reality right now," Adam exclaimed.

"Yes," said Socrates.

"Then, what are we waiting for?" Adam said excitedly. "Let's go find my father."

Socrates spoke softly. "You don't know everything yet, Adam. You don't know that Chronos will do everything in his power to keep this truth from you. You will be his prey. He will try to destroy you. But you need to remember you hold the key to defeating him within. Call on Kairos simply by sitting quietly no matter what else is going on. And she will help." He stopped speaking for a moment, then put his arm around Adam.

"But I can't go along this time, Adam, This is your journey alone."

"Can Sophie come along?" Adam asked.

"Not this time, Adam. This is your journey. Sophie can stay here and we will wait for you to return."

"But how shall I get there?"

"Find a place to sit and rest your eyes and concentrate on where you want to go first else you will end up some place else. Just stay focused and the way will open before you." Socrates called Sophie to his side and walked away. Adam spotted an old oak tree not far away and walked to it where he sat down, closed his eyes, and thought only of his destination.

A Teacher, His Students, and the Great Questions of Life

(5)

Adam slowly opened his eyes, but he couldn't see anything at all. It was pitch black. He felt quite alone, and it was cold. He hugged himself to keep warm, afraid to know where he was. In the distance he thought he spotted a small light. As he watched, the light grew closer and he began to hear a moaning sound grow until he had to cover his ears. He closed his eyes for a few seconds because the light was hurting them. But when he opened them in front of him stood a horrid creature, blood dripping from his mouths. He had many heads and claws, in which he was carrying many clocks, each one ticking in unison.

"Who comes to my forest to disturb my work?" There were many voices speaking together, as if part of a chorus, but sounding very much like the ticking of many clocks.

"I came here to find my father," Adam said softly.

"Speak up," bellowed the voices. "I can't hear you with all the ticking."

"I came to find my father," repeated Adam.

"And who are you?" the voices responded.

"I am Adam."

Lightning and thunder sounded in the distance. "What? A time creature comes to my den of randomness where only I live? Did you not see the sign when you came into my kingdom: *No Mortals Permitted Beyond This Point*? Do you not understand that once here you can never return to the Land of Time? You are in a black hole where neither time nor space exists. By all rights you are not here at all." With that the creature drew closer.

What Is Time?

"I may not be here at all," said Adam. "I was just concentrating, trying to find my father. And here I am." Adam felt himself shivering.

"So you may not be here at all except as some kind of experiment? I suppose I should congratulate you. No one has broken the thin veil which separated us from the mortal dimension for centuries. You must be a very powerful wizard."

"I beg your pardon," Adam said, "but I am not a wizard, only a small boy looking for his father." He paused and in spite of his fears, looked at the creature in front of him. "And who are you?"

The voices responded in a loud voice, the words roll down the mountains and spilling into the forest. "I am Chronos, the keeper of time, the one who destroys all who seek to live forever. I have been called many names throughout your mortal history—Shiva, the Goddess, the Watch Maker, the Power of Darkness and Death."

"Then you are what we all fear," said Adam.

"Yes, but I am not all bad. Think what it would be like if there were not death, if everyone lived forever? Your planet would have long disappeared, sunk under the weight of its own populations. My work is to destroy but also to create, to get rid of the old so that the new might emerge."

"You don't scare me," said Adam. "I don't think you as bad as you want me to think you are." As Adam watched, the horrid creature he had first seen melted into a small white cloud.

"You see," said the cloud, "I am not the horrid creature you feared. It's all how you perceive me. You mortals think too much about differences instead of seeing that differences have a fundamental unity. You can't have heat without cold, winter without fall, and all the rest. Now I am the one who brings relief. I am not your enemy."

Adam touched the white cloud. "Are you still Chronos?"

"Yes, but with a different face. I call this face Kairos, a face of kindness and compassion for all mortals; the face of a power which lets you see beyond time into what is timeless."

"Then you can help me find my father?" asked Adam.

"No I can't remove the veil so you can see him, but I can give you something to use so you can." With that the cloud melted into a new form, a smooth, black stone from the riverbed. "Here," said the cloud, "is a magical stone. It contains within it all the powers of the universe. All you need do is keep rubbing it and repeating your deepest wish."

"And will I see my father?" Adam questioned.

"Just rub me and close your eyes," the stone said as it floated into Adam's hands.

Adam sat down and began to rub the stone. "I want to see my father. I want to see my father. I want to see my father." He closed his eyes and kept repeating the same words.

It seemed a very long time to Adam but in truth only a few minutes had passed since he began rubbing the stone. When he slowly opened his eyes he was startled to see how bright the colors had become of the land around him. The green was the deepest green he had ever seen, the blue flowers in the field vivid, the sky brighter blue still. He could hear the sounds of the river rushing in the distance and the chirping of birds in the trees. "This is truly heaven if there is a heaven," Adam spoke softly.

What Is Time?

"Not heaven, just another photo from the great book of life," a bird spoke from the branch of a tree. "You're just seeing things for the first time. You've always had the chance to do this, but someone had to show the way. Now you are here. What do you want?"

"I want to find my father," Adam replied.

"But he is always here. It's you who are missing." The bird flew down and perched on Adam's shoulder. "It you want to find your father, here's what I would do; but, of course, I am just another figment of your imagination, so what do I know about what you think is the real world? "

"I'm listening," Adam said. "Just let me know what you advise."

"Okay," said the bird. "Go back to where you started and find Sophie and Socrates and begin to walk along the path in front of you. Sometimes the only way to begin is to begin all over again, but take a few friends along. If you focus your mind the pathway will open before you and you and your friends can walk through."

"That sounds too simple. Why didn't I think of this before?" Adam questioned.

"The path was always in front you. You just had to use your imagination to find it." The bird flew away and Adam closed his eyes and imagined being with Socrates and Sophie where he had left them, which now seemed more than years than hours ago.

He awoke to blackness. Or was he still dreaming? This felt like a bad dream, a nightmare. He was falling. What would happen if he hit the ground? He knew without being told he was dropping into the Void, a black hole in the midst of the stars, where he remembered hearing there was no time or space and if you fell into one you would be lost forever. But he felt himself collapsing into the arms of someone or something and his drop stopped.

"Where am I?" he asked.

"For now with me," said a strange voice seemingly coming from everywhere around him. "Remember me?"

"Not really," Adam replied, "although your voice does sound familiar. Do you think you could speak softer so I don't get a headache?"

"Is this better?" A softer voice came out of the blackness. "I am Chronos, the keeper of time, the black hole itself," the voice continued.

"Yes, I remember you now," Adam responded, "but I thought you were gone. In any case, I know you are not to be feared. You can turn into a better time if you and I so choose." Adam was quiet for a moment before speaking again. "But I was headed back to Socrates and Sophie to choose a path to find my father. Why am I here?"

"You are not ready yet," Chronos responded, "until you have heard a few more things."

"And what might these be?" Adam asked.

Chronos turned his face and became Kairos. "Perhaps you can hear me better this way when you are not so afraid." A warm breeze seemed to fill the void and a gentle voice spoke.

"Adam, it's all about time, everything. And I do mean everything. So hear me out—it's a long lesson and I want you to pay attention." Kairos suddenly appeared before him, this time as young child about Adam's age.

"Let's try this on for size; perhaps being your age may help you focus on my words, not my appearance. Ready or not, here comes the lesson."

"You see, in the very beginning, before there was anything in this universe, there were other universes already

What Is Time?

in existence, some of them strung on a string like bubbles. These was no life in the universe you live in now, only the possibility of life. This was what I call the Before Time period. And when one of the older universes spilled over into the Void, your universe began—not as a big bang but like a school bell reverberating, actually still sounding today but only your dog can hear. And when your universe began, so did Chronos, time itself—at least time as you measure by your clocks."

Kairos paused. "Do you understand thus far, Adam?"

"Yes, I think so," Adam replied.

"Once there was time, everything changed and the void took shape and exploded, forming new worlds beyond what even your greatest telescopes can see today. The explosion hurtled everything outward until it touched another black hole; but it kept pushing. For how long, no one knows. Perhaps it keeps pushing until it runs out of energy and begins to collapse and the whole process begins anew. But no mind, time began and you began, too, and over time you began to measure it, but of course all your measurements were simply crude devices to find Chronos. But Chronos just was there; you didn't need to do anything. But you tried. You kept pushing and probing time to find more—actually to escape your condition—creatures imprisoned in time. But you couldn't, no matter how hard you tried. You even invented religions which promised you would live forever, but they really didn't know how to defeat time. They just used this promise to control you and to get your money, of course. That is why this period is called Trapped in Time. Because you were trapped in bodies, which would eventually run down. Even your great civilizations would eventually disappear. You spent thousands of years and countless lives trying to overcome Chronos, which goes by another name—death. And no matter how hard you tried, you never read won the battle with time. You were stuck in your prison and couldn't get out."

"That's a sad story," Adam said quietly. "It makes it all seem so hopeless. Eventually nothing will remain and time will be no more and since we are trapped in time that means we will cease to exist, too."

"But that's not the end of the story," Kairos said. "There is another chapter you haven't heard yet. It's what is called The Beyond Time period."

"Beyond time? What's that supposed to mean? Are you taking about what my grandpa called 'heaven?' He used to tell me that if I loved Jesus and did the right thing, that's where I was going."

"Heaven? That's not a place, Adam; it's another dimension. And you hold the keys to getting there. What you call heaven is just another dimension that's always bumping into you. You're just attuned to Chronos too much in your world, but there is another world, too."

"I don't understand," Adam said.

"Let me tell you a story about your father. He understood. When he was a young man he went on a journey to find his ancestors in an old country across the sea from where he lived. He didn't find his ancestors, but he did find something far more important. You see one early morning he went for a walk up a small hill and when he got tired, he rested under an old oak tree and dozed off. Somewhere between being asleep and being awake he had a great awakening and realized that there was another dimension bumping into his right then. Later he described it as a veil separating his world from another, a thin place he called it, and if one could realize that they might see

What Is Time?

through the veil to another dimension. And you called that dimension heaven, but it's not really a place at all, but a state of mind you can discover whenever you pause long enough to peek through the veil."

Kairos stopped speaking. Adam was very still.

"I'm not sure I get all this, but one thing that does make sense to me is that my father is still alive in some other dimension and that if I can see through the veil, I can see him, and if learn how I can really go to that other dimension and speak with him again. Do I have it right?"

"Yes," said Kairos. "Now you need to practice making the journey. I know you can do it. Keep my words in your heart and trust them."

"So, that's it, right?" Adam asked. "You're really done teaching me?"

"Well I did the best I could. Chronos is the keeper of time so he is really the storyteller in time. Don't you know he always begins his stories by saying: 'Once upon a time'? It's his way of getting your attention. Stories are what draw children in because they can suspend their doubts long enough to listen; adults need charts and graphs and numbers.

Adam felt the blackness receding and in the distance thought he heard the sound of school bell in the distance. "I'm very tired again and need some time to rest."

(6)

Where am I now? It is dark and quiet here except for a stomach rumbling in the distance. I cannot see anything. But I know something great is about to happen. All I can think is that I much prefer to stay here.

Where did I come from? Who was I before I can to this place or was I still Adam? Where are other people? Where the trees and flowers and blue sky?

Get me out here!

Whoops. Here I come, ready or not!

It's a warm night as a breeze blows in from my bedroom window. I begin to cry. Suddenly I hear her voice. "There, there, Adam. I'm here."

She is the one who cares for me. I don't know her name, but I carry the memory of her face inside. I cannot speak with words. only make myself heard by crying.

Suddenly there is another presence in the room, this one less familiar. The voice is deeper but I know it well. "Sorry, I would have gotten up and come in so you can sleep," the voice says.

"It's alright," the softer voice replies. "I wonder, do babies dream?"

"What a question at this time of the night," the second voice responds. "You will turn this child into a philosopher if you carry on with this."

"Children are full of questions once they have the words to express them," the other voice responds. She picks me up gently and pats my back. I burp and fall asleep on her shoulder.

"Adam, did you hear my question?" He glanced up to see Miss Medcalf, book in hand, walking down the row of desks and standing in front of his. "I asked you a question

What Is Time?

about the reading assignment for today. Why did Captain Ahab want to kill the white whale?"

He was quiet. Miss Medcalf glanced down at him and said in a low voice: "Adam, see me after class today."

He waited all day, worried about what Miss Medcalf might say. But as he stood by her desk after the last school bell had rung, her words were kind:

"Adam, I know it's been difficult for you coming to a new school and you don't know many of the other children yet. But I've really enjoyed the stories you write and I have a suggestion for you—would you be willing to share them with the class? I know that might be hard because you are a new pupil here, but I think your stories are wonderful and need to be heard."

And so the following week, after Miss Medcalf asked him to read one of his stories to the class, he began doing so and continued every Wednesday at the opening of each class. It was the beginning of what he suspected would take him a whole lifetime of storytelling.

He is in the school cafeteria hoping Jenny doesn't sit down next to him. But she brings her tray and sits across from him. She smiles but doesn't say anything. Now what should I do, he says to himself? Should I keep my eyes down, eat fast, and leave? Should I look at her and say hello? This feels very strange.

Luckily I don't have to say anything. She opens a milk carton and looks at me. "Can you believe our teacher giving us all that homework for tomorrow?" She is now looking directly at me. I feel my face turning red. No words form. I shake my head and keep eating.

"Anyway, I hate math and now I have to take the book home tonight and work on some algebra. What a drag." She rolls her eyes. They are a lovely shade of green. I still feel tongue-tied.

She unwraps a piece of pie from her tray and continues. "Say, Adam, why don't we sit together during study hall time and work on the math? If we put our heads together we might not have to take any work home tonight.

"What'd you say?"

I shake my head up and down, hoping I don't appear too eager. After all, I hate math. But there's something about Jenny that makes me want to work on an algebra problem with her. "See you after lunch," she says, as I watch her walking away, her blue skirt swaying in the light.

It's the end of my senior year in college and after four years of frolic, fun and occasional studying, I wonder what I will do after graduation. I've been studying philosophy but no one wants to hire a philosopher. Most cause too much trouble, like my hero Socrates who questioned the gods of his age and supposedly damaged young minds with his teachings. I don't want to end up like that.

So what do I do? I have only a few months before they toss me out of this safe haven with a piece of paper saying I graduated but with no prospects of future employment.

One of my favorite professors gave us a lesson this past week, and it's one that might help me understand my life journey. He asked us to take out a piece of paper and complete this sentence: I was put on earth to _____. I tried, I really tried to finish it, but the harder I tried the worse it got, and at the end I rolled the paper into a small ball and tossed it in the nearest

What Is Time?

waste paper can. My teacher frowned. Some of my classmates laughed. I bet if they were honest with themselves, they would do the same thing.

"You're doing a great job, Adam. Thanks."

The speaker was my boss, the city editor of the local paper and I am his star reporter. I know now why I was put on earth—to take words and make people laugh or cry, to get their attention. It's where I started out in grade school and where I have ended up for the last twenty years. Now I know how to finish the sentence I couldn't complete in college: I was put on earth to be a writer.

It may be only a newspaper with a small readership, but the joy I feel inside when I see a story or column I have written is about as close to heaven as I will ever get.

One day my editor tells me there won't be newspapers. Everything will be electronic. Unless you can get electronic ink on the hands and do battle with editors about stories you want to write, I'd prefer to stay just where I am.

Now where am I? And where were Socrates and Sophie? And why was the sound of the school bell so close? He peered down and saw he was holding the hand of a small boy.

"Dad, hurry up, I'm going to be late for class."

Why was this child calling him Dad and who was he? For that matter, he thought to himself: Who am I? He looked down at his hands and feet; they weren't the hands and feet of a boy, but of a man.

"Dad, did you hear me? We need to hurry up."

A Teacher, His Students, and the Great Questions of Life

This was getting very strange indeed. He knew he was Adam still, but in a larger body. But who was the boy?

"Dad, I'm going to run ahead. It's only a half block. I'll see you after school." With that the boy raced ahead.

It's very dark. I think there may be people around me but their voices grow dim. I try to open my eyes to see my wife. She is crying. My son is holding her hand.

So this is it, huh? The end, the terminus, the conclusion or whatever you want to call it is now. And I disappear or go to the Great Perhaps. Maybe I will see my father and mother again, speak with Miss Medcalf, pet Sophie. I don't want to go but I know I must. It is time. Ready or not, here I come!

I am resting on the grass, surrounded by trees and flowers. In the distance I think I hear people laughing. Where am I?

"Outside clock time," a voice answers. "Don't you understand yet? Time is millions of zones, chapters if you wish, and you inhabit only a tiny portion of them, one at a time, with others. Who you are with in each chapter and what you choose to do equals your book of life."

I feel a kindly presence close by. "I am your father. Would I lie to you?"

He holds my hand as we walk down the road toward an old man and dog waiting just over the horizon. If this isn't heaven, I don't know what is.

Thirteen

A Teacher's Story

(Note: If narrative philosophy is about stories, mine, yours and the great tale of the humanity on this planet, then it is fitting that this book close with mine—what it means to be a teacher, not so say I am so different from others but that I am very much the same—plots, characters and often outcomes. As I near the end of my life, I felt it important to include my story as the ending of this book. Hopefully in my story you will find something of yourself and can forgive my shortcomings and celebrate my small victories.)

I'VE BEEN TEACHING FOR a long time, whether in college classrooms, pulpits, newspapers, magazines or wherever I might be. Getting out of graduate school with a master's degree in philosophy, I found no demand for philosophers, so went to work as a journalist and part-time professor, introducing the subject to unsuspecting community college students. For the past ten years I've been teaching philosophy, first at a community college and then at a four-year liberal arts school.

It was at the community college that a student struggling with the dissolution of her marriage, shrinking funds, and two children to feed, asked me what good philosophy might be. "Will it feed my children?" she

A Teacher, His Students, and the Great Questions of Life

asked. I wanted to respond as only a philosopher might with a question to combat hers: "Well, not food on the table, perhaps, but food for the mind." Luckily I stopped myself before speaking and making myself sound like a television commercial, and waited for her to continue.

Holding the thick textbook for my course in her hands, she pointed to it and remarked: "Look at this textbook the college requires us to buy and read. It costs over a hundred dollars and you and I each know I won't read a quarter of it for this course. Think how much food I might buy for that amount. And I certainly know how much you complain about its cost and bulkiness. So why must I read it just because some department chair requires all philosophy faculty to use this book? How can this person know how students learn when he stopped teaching a few decades ago? I mean, what's it all about Dr. J? Is it about us learning—or the course requirements of the department?"

I felt saddened by the student's comments, embarrassed even by the question about the choice of an expensive textbook, realizing that here I was teaching in an inner city community college where most students had little money or time and I was following the rule someone else made years ago that every philosophy teacher was required to use the same over priced textbook. So I asked myself the question I had often used before: What Would Socrates Do (WWSD)? And the answer was clear—if the expensive text does not help students learn and, in fact, leaves them bored or confused, ask them for feedback. So I took a radical step: I asked students what they thought about the book and our time together. What I learned from them changed by life and my teaching style. They told me that what they loved and learned in our time together had nothing to do with the textbooks or my lectures but with the opportunities I gave them to tell their stories, listen to those of other students, and learn how to engage in real dialog. And they related something else, too, that at first made me wonder how I got three graduate degrees and never learned—they valued me most as a coach or mentor in the class, a member of a learning community in other words. The truth was that this was the very process probably employed by those students in the schools of philosophy in Athens, Greece, many centuries ago. These budding thinkers were not studying philosophy; they were doing it, becoming philosophers in the process. It substantiated my view that my role was to enable others to practice philosophy in a safe and challenging environment, that in this class which met for three hours a week we were recreating the ancient art of learning how to think by using our own lives as textbooks and each other as tutors. And rather than being the chief lecturer who poured my information into slits in the backs of their heads to be regurgitated back on final exams, I was one learner among others, just another philosopher-in-the-making, someone trying to make sense out of my life and all the questions which came from living. From that moment on, I chose to treat philosophy as a practical discipline helping all of us in the classroom community learn more about ourselves, each other, and the great questions that plagued humankind since first we etched drawings on cave walls. I think I rekindled my love of learning. And I learned that made me a better teacher.

One semester I tossed my lecture notes out, posting them on a course online resource along with video lectures if anyone wanted to remember the "good old days," when the learned professor spent fifty-five minutes telling students what he or she had learned in graduate school, watching them scribble notes and never look up, and saving five minutes at the end of each class for questions. Of course, after nearly an hour of hearing a lecture, most students might be asleep with their eyes still open, mentally gone, or fantasizing about the coed in the next seat.

But it dawned on me that after two masters and one doctoral degree, no one had helped me figured out how to teach. Yes, I thought I knew what to teach. Hadn't I kept all my course notes and used them for years afterward, their faded yellow pages reminders of past times? I remember now my first class and the lesson I should have learned then, but didn't. It was an introductory philosophy class at a community college. I had spent hours preparing for the lecture, retyping notes from the first course in philosophy I had taken in graduate school. I even dressed the part—bow tie, blue button down shirt, brown tweed coat, khaki pants, dark rimmed glasses, and white sneakers. I smoked a pipe in those days and kept it stuffed in my coat pocket where students could see it, thus confirming that while I looked like I was eighteen years old I was, in fact, old enough to puff on a pipe. I hoped to convince them as I walked into the room that I was the professor, the learned doctor, the giver of all knowledge, he-who-must-be-respected. I'll show those kids what a real professor does, I thought to myself.

As I sauntered down the hallway, books under my arm, I headed to Room 102, prepared for the first time to face my students. I opened the door at precisely 9 am. knowing the students would be waiting for me and prepared to give a first impression that would last a semester. But as

What Is Time?

I entered the classroom, I tripped—my books, notebook and pipe flying across the floor, as I desperately sought to catch my glasses which slid off the bridge of my nose and dangled there for everyone to observe. There was a hush in the room, a few students muffled giggles cutting through the silence. My face turned red as I bent down to pick up the papers and pipe, then staggered toward the lectern (which I held on to for dear life fearing I might fall again). The silence made the situation worse. If I had been wiser or surer of myself, I would have laughed and encouraged the students to do the same. But I was too focused on appearances, straightening my tie and tucking my pipe into the jacket pocket. And there I lectured for a time, not taking my eyes off my notes or my hands off the table. It was one of the worst moments of my life, and I wish I could say I learned something from the experience. I was too young and inexperienced to know myself well. The first advice of the Oracle of Delphi in ancient Greece was to know yourself. Three graduate degrees in philosophy never helped much with this advice, so I did what had been advised by my faculty mentor—developed good lectures, stuck to them, and limited discussion to the final minutes of class time.

At the end of that first philosophy class, the final humiliation came from a very young student, the last to leave the room, who said quietly to me on the way out: "You didn't hurt yourself, did you?" Then I realized that what these students would remember for a long time was not what I said, but what happened to me—and that story would be told and embellished for years to come. No one ever mentioned this episode to me, but I walked quietly down the hallways expecting snickers or giggles and keeping my eyes as close to the ground as I did now in the classroom, reading my lecture notes and seldom looking at the students. This experience later taught me the most important thing about life, including being a teacher: It's about relationships, not degrees or books or lectures, and I learned as much from the relationships as the students I thought I was teaching. The truth is they were teaching me.

And so I turned away from teaching full time and instead did other things with my life—becoming a reporter and writer, a community activist, a minister, and from time to time an occasional teacher. But, of course, once a teacher, always a teacher. It was my calling, not just a job. And so, ten years ago, semi-retired, I started writing and teaching philosophy part time, first at a community college and then at a four-year liberal arts school. I returned to the old tactic of giving lectures, showing how much I really was like most people who try the same things more than once expecting but not getting different results. I was setting myself up again for being bored and boring others. I was afraid to be myself and let others be themselves. It was too risky, almost chaotic, and I was still not ready.

I must admit I didn't change all at once. It took time for me to try new ways of teaching and learning. I had to learn about myself, who I was and not just what I taught. I structured class time now to wonder, question, be silly, and struggle with our lives and questions, my own included. I was understanding now that learning was about teaching one another, not just pouring information into the slits in the backs of student heads. One day I tossed the big expensive textbook in a wastepaper can, and heard back from a college administrator that my actions were "unprofessional." I responded that Socrates suffered

What Is Time?

the scorn of people in his time and hoped she wouldn't ask me to drink hemlock and die, as Socrates was forced to do. She shook her head but didn't smile; she realized that my classes were always full and that translated into money for the college. So she turned the other way and I turned to learning what worked.

It was in one class where students were learning and actually having fun doing so but wondered why they needed the large textbook when it wasn't used that things started to change. I had helped them figure out how to recoup this investment in the book by selling it to students in other classes who had to read it. They reminded me of what I often said to me that their lives were the textbooks and they were the writers. They challenged me to write a book that mirrored what we were doing in the classroom that wouldn't exceed two hundred pages or cost more than twenty dollars. It took me a year, but I did. The students loved the new book because it gave them and me more time to talk in class. A few faculty later wondered if the book were academically worthy of their institution. "Ask the students who have used this book," was all I could respond.

A year later after teaching another introductory ethics class, a student approached me afterward. I had found him to be one of the brightest students in my classes and someone who struggled in a deep way with the kinds of perplexing questions philosophers raise but seldom answer. He had heard me say at the beginning of this class that students brought the textbook with them to every class—themselves, and that I believed that what the ancient oracle of Delphi told Socrates was the most important thing to know was as important today as it was over two centuries ago: *Know thyself.* "So, how does one go about knowing himself?" he asked. I think I stammered for a minute. The question was so obvious I wondered how I had missed it myself, and it was broader than just knowing about yourself—it was knowing about others, indeed the cosmos itself. I am not sure what else I said to him that day, but over the weeks to come he kept asking the same question and coming at his responses in many ways, almost as if he were in dialog with himself. And when the semester ended, that's about what he said he had discovered—knowing himself required him to stay awake, sharpen the questions and his responses, until he arrived at his own responses, which I found not altogether different from my own. He said I had advised him "to lean into the questions," and that's what he had done. And that's what I propose to do for as long as I can learn and teach in a classroom—lean into my own questions and hope my responses trigger others.

It took more money and time and memorization than I care to remember to realize that I have arrived where I started many decades ago and finally found who I am and why I am sitting here tonight a few minutes before a new class starts, wondering who will join this community of learning, and excited I am to be waiting for yet another experience. I am finally a teacher who loves to be in a community of learning, and will remain so until someone has to carry me out of the classroom. It's times like tonight I realize that my goal of creating a real learning community in which there is no longer the traditional separations between teacher and those taught are realized. I can't hide behind the podium or point to a visual presentation on the screen. They've called me out and if

What Is Time?

I don't respond, I violate my own understanding of what learning is about. So I have to come clean, maybe not with all the sordid dimensions of my own life, but at least letting them know I have been where many of them have been and somehow or other made it like many of them have.

So to answer one curious student about how I became a teacher, here's the short version of how one teacher influenced me in fourth grade.

In my earliest years of schooling I attended an experimental school run by the university. Thee desks were not in straight rows, the teacher often worked around or sat on the ground with us, we shared stories and music and games, and we began each day with a few moments of silence. As I think about this now, I realize that much of what I do in my classes reflects these early experiences. I may not recall everything that happened in that school, but the happy feelings about being there have lasted. That is, until my family moved and I transferred to a typical suburban school. There, all the desks were in neat rows. We sat and only spoke after we raised our hands. The books were boring and hard to read. It was a traumatic time in my life.

But then something happened that changed my life. It wasn't any great or life shattering event. My fourth grade teacher knew my story and had been watching me. She could see I was not happy. One day after school ended, she took me aside. She had all of us write stories and keep them in our big notebook (which I still have today). She told me how much she enjoyed the writing and wondered if I would be willing to read them out loud to the students each morning to begin the day. It was a little scary for me, but I worked up the nerve and started the next day.

A Teacher, His Students, and the Great Questions of Life

Day after day I kept reading my stories. And I needed more to tell, I wrote more, until I had a thick notebook. I still retain memories of those days.

When there was a teacher-parent conference, my teacher told my parents about how much she and the children loved my stories. And when my father said that being a writer or preacher was part of my family heritage, my teacher responded: "Yes, but I think we also have a budding teacher in our midst because Johnny also loves to share his stories with others." My mother, a frustrated actress who loved to do what she called "dramatic readings" most have been quite pleased. I thank my fourth grade teacher for planting the seed of being a teacher, and I blame my father for pointing the way toward being a minister. Well, actually, I don't really blame my father; I simply thought that coming from a family of many generations of ministers, I was expected to follow. I tried that path for nearly a quarter century, and I was never comfortable. I felt I was playing a role in a drama I didn't write. Maybe Ralph Waldo Emerson knew my feelings when he left the parish and said it was the better part of person which didn't want to be a minister to keep humble.

My break with parish ministry came one night when I got back to my church office after visiting a parishioner. It was late and I was tired when a woman of the night (the church was a few blocks away from a red light district in the city) approached. "Want to have some fun?" she asked seductively. I responded without thinking: "No thanks. I can't. I'm headed to church." She walked away. I walked away that year from the ministry. I had told myself the truth as I felt it. When my friends ask why I am no longer a minister, I respond: "A prostitute changed my life." They usually don't ask for more details.

What Is Time?

For the past decade I have been teaching or, better yet, learning. I knew the first moment I stepped back into a classroom that this was where I was supposed to be. It was Aristotle's arete, his view that the purpose of being a human being is to flourish, to be all one is supposed to be. I suppose most of this was due to timing. I had tried teaching when I was young, but was too self-conscious to be myself. In my later years, I knew more about myself and was less anxious about what others felt. Perhaps teaching is more about learning about oneself and being congruent with that self-understanding than having the right pedagogical approach.

Am I a teacher who writes or a writer who teaches? I still am not sure. If I am honest with myself, I believe it is learning to live with both, teaching and writing being part of the same life mission—to seek and communicate what it means to be a human being. But in these later years of my life, I find joy in teaching more than anything else I do.

That's my story, boys and girls, and I have not yet written the last chapter. I have a few more years to go, but I will need to be carried out of the classroom before I leave teaching. Sometimes I have students write what they want on their tombstones as an exercise in focusing on how they want to be remembered. I confess I want to be cremated and instead of a stone have an old parking meter placed in the ground with the words EXPIRED showing through the glass and a note which suggests they can still put coins in the slot but these will be given to the local homeless shelter. Surely this a better way to leave something of worth behind than an expensive tombstone.

A Teacher, His Students, and the Great Questions of Life

I am not sure what case Arthur Conan Doyle was handling at the time he wrote that Sherlock Holmes thought flowers were the surest sign of providence or whether by some stroke of fortune he simply had a moment to smell the roses in an English country garden, but I do know that gardens are like outdoor altars where you can sit quietly and see life throwing off its winter garments and poking its head through the thawing earth.

I come from a long line of Welsh and English gardeners. Though I grew up in Philadelphia, I can still remember the garden outside our back window and the return of the same turtle every year to a batch of high grass near the drain pipe. Even then, concrete walls and traffic notwithstanding, spring came as a joyful surprise every year, reminding me that all life seeks to move toward the light, if given half a chance.

There are some places this year where I imagine spring will come slowly: in foreign lands torn by wars or in some of our own neighborhoods where dreams die sometimes harsh and way too early. Raised a Calvinist I expect the worst, but can now see hope rise every spring with the first sign of daffodils or the sound of a bat hitting a ball into the outfield.

You can learn a great deal by sitting near a garden. If nothing else, you will be able to refrain from causing other people more problems.

There is something humbling about planting a garden, especially for a city slicker like myself. You toss a few bulbs in before winter and, presto, without so much as lifting a shovel or rake, the green shoots come bursting out of the earth, which had been so barren and cold for so long. Talk about the simple graces of life—nothing equals

What Is Time?

the sight of yellow and blue and red and orange sending their flares into the sunlight.

I also understand more why diversity is beautiful from studying my garden. The blue flowers do not say to the red, "Get out of here, this is our spot on the earth!" The orange do not seize the green buds by the stems and try to toss them out of their spaces. The beauty of a garden is that each flower retains its uniqueness, but when joined together with others forms a beautiful patchwork tapestry. Stand back a few feet when your garden is in full bloom and observe its majesty, just as marvelous as seeing the blue planet earth from the distance of the moon.

There is an old proverb: "Many things grow in the garden that were never sowed there." That's the really humbling part of tending to a garden and a life as well.. No matter how carefully you plant the seeds, a few weeds always manage to grow. You can't order then around any more than you can control the people around you. And, sometimes, even weeds add a touch of green to a flower patch or a crack in the city sidewalk.

Amid the sounds of bombs and planes and conflicts, a garden, like poetry, draws us inward to some magical place we thought lost in childhood. And the news is good: Life renews itself. To that, we can all say, "Amen."

In a way I could not imagined after I stumbled back into teaching college students about themselves, which is usually what I claimed we were doing in philosophy classes, I have come to discover the classroom is my learning garden—a place to grow ideas, water the ground of the curious mind, identify and even appreciate the weeds and nurture the glorious bursting colors of maturing hearts. It's what it means to be a teacher to me, this chance to grow souls, minds, and hearts. It's an art one learns by practice. The only way to become a teacher is to stand with others who are learning as you are.

(Portions of this appeared first in the Friends Journal, May 1,, 2004, and is used with permission. For more information: www.friendsjournal.org)

I have come to believe that the human enterprise is most vividly understood by telling and listening to stories. We are the makers, tellers, and sometimes listeners of stories. We and the universe itself began as a story that had a plot, major and minor characters, conflicts, victories and defeats, and sometimes a surprise ending. Stories are what keep us human, although even trees or rocks have stories all their own, told in tongues other than human language. One story has more than one meaning, even to the one who tells it. But we store energy in a story like a battery cell; it is the story which invigorates us and leads to what some say is "soul." And some would add that many of the early teachers of wisdom saw philosophy as a therapy for the soul, a way of clearing out false ideas and seeking truth for how best to live.

One of the first exercises I have students do in my courses is to compile his or her book of life in which they look at their lives in terms of seven year chapters, jot a few notes in each chapter to trigger their memories to tell their stories in small groups formed in the class. It surprised me how many never had thought of their lives as a book of stories, unique to each one but with common themes shared with many others. Every student, like every person, has a story and most have never told it to others, at least heard over many years. Initially some are fearful of doing so in a small group, but once comfortable

What Is Time?

with others and knowing their stories will be held in confidence, learn to tell their life story and listen to those of others. And I almost always need to break up their time together because they don't want to stop.

I am not sure why I should have been surprised that people need to tell and hear stories; after all, storytelling was the first means of communication for building a sense of being part of something greater than oneself. There are days when I think the best I might do as a teacher is offer a space where people might come together to tell and share their stories, and then get out of the way or join one of the storytelling groups myself. Perhaps this really is what religion was before it got crammed into buildings and led by specialists.

I usually share with students a model or paradigm for showing the various dimensions of stories. Pointing to someone in the front row, I say life is about my story, her story, our story (pointing to the entire class), and the great stories or myths from many traditions. I know as soon as I use the word *myth* I need to clarify what I mean. A myth is not true in the sense a mathematical equation is true; a myth contains truths for living that are difficult to convey as strict formulas. A myth points beyond itself to some greater meaning, often one too deep for our limited language. And then I launch into one of the great myths or stories from Jewish tradition—the story of our origins on this planet, which began in a garden, the scene for paradise.

I ask the students how many believe there was an Adam or Eve. A few say they do believe. Some snicker when they hear others say so. Many know the names of Adam or Eve but forget the story. So I tell it, not always exactly as it was written in the book of Genesis, but close enough to get the essential features. Sometimes I tell the students if they are tired, to close their eyes and listen, and if they are good, I might have cookies and milk after the story. And often I do offer these when the story is over.

I begin as most stories start: "Once upon a time, a long time ago, God was lonely and wanted someone else around to appreciate the universe. And so Adam was created and he also got lonely. So God gave him a sleeping pill and while he was asleep, took out a rib and created a woman, Eve. And God put them in a wonderful garden with everything they needed. It was perfect. But as you surely know yourselves, we're restless creatures and always are dissatisfied with things even if they are perfect. So Adam and Eve were bored and wanted to have as much power as God."

A few students by now are smiling, at least the ones who know the original version and realize I am updating the story. "So that's why men are always a rib short of a full body and one brain short of intelligence," one female student said. "Come on, teach is not telling it because it's true. He's making it up."

"Let's not take it literally for now," I countered, although I got them wondering by asking men and then women to cut the number of ribs each had. One student offered to count the ribs on the coed who sat next to him, but I said no. So I continued with the story. "So God puts a tree in the middle of the garden and tells them not to eat any fruit on the tree. And what do you suppose they do?"

"They eat it, of course, because there wasn't any fast food joint nearby," one student quipped, looking around at his friends to appreciate his wit.

What Is Time?

"Well, you are right. A serpent in the garden tempts Eve and Adam to eat the fruit, saying if they do they will be as gods, knowing the difference between good and evil."

"So it was the woman who caused this mess? I knew it. Same today. It's always the woman messing up my life." The young man shook his head back and forth as if agreeing with himself.

"Okay, okay, let me finish the story and then we'll talk about it," I said. "So Adam eats the fruit and God comes walking in the garden asking what happened. God already knew beforehand what would happen, which is a n interesting theological issue for later—so if God knew beforehand, then the those two folk in the garden had no choice. Anyway, Adam blames Eve. Eve blames the serpent. And the poor serpent has no one to blame, so God makes him crawl on the ground."

I pause and look out at the blank looks on the faces. "So what's it all mean?" I ask and wait.

At first no one says anything. Then the responses start coming like ripples in a pond. "Damn women, always tempting us . . . .Don't believe that story really is true . . . .If that man hadn't eaten the apple they'd still be there . . . .So if God knew beforehand, then Adam and Eve weren't to blame, right . . . .Man, couldn't God have made things so perfect nothing bad would ever have happened."

I wait until the room gets quiet again. "So, here's the point I want to make: With any story you can ask two questions: First, is it true? Or second, what truths does the story convey? You see, I don't believe there literally was an Adam and Eve in the garden, but I don't stop there. I ask what the story might mean, and then I come up with something different. It's a story about who we are

A Teacher, His Students, and the Great Questions of Life

and what makes us humans. Think about it, we want to be gods, to know everything; we try, but fail. And here's the part of the story that means something more: Adam blames Eve; Eve blames the serpent. So each scapegoats the other; they don't take responsibility for their own decisions or actions. And that's a description of the human story—yours, mine, and everyone. Think of the holocaust and how certain groups were unfairly blamed for social ills. It's the old story in new situations. And that is what philosophy seeks to do—interpret the meanings of stories, past and present, yours and mine, and whole societies. Why? To offer us guides for living. Philosophy, after all, means simply the *love of wisdom*." The class ends. Students still are talking.

In one of the first introductory philosophy courses I ever taught a student who had been struggling with the subject approached me after class. "I don't get it," he said. "I like being in class and learning, but this textbook is complicated and confusing, and when I try to read it I wish we were back in class and I could ask everyone else what they thought." I knew this student was bright and interested in ideas. In class he was usually asking the best questions to help the rest of us. I wondered what I was doing wrong, which is the first thing any teacher asks when encountering a student having problems, instead of asking him what might help. He beat me to the punch, however. "I think what you said in class today about philosophy being a practical subject to help us live and think deeper makes sense to me, but how do we go about living and thinking more deeply? It's certainly not in the textbook. I don't remember what I read in it an hour or so later.

What Is Time?

But you said that you believe we learn by doing, not just thinking. You called it orthopraxis, not orthodoxy, remember?" I was thrilled he remembered that orthopraxis was about the right practice, not just the right belief as in orthodoxy. "Tell you what," I said, "the next class we will try something different."

Class day loomed sooner than I thought and when the students gathered in the room I asked them to pick up their books and backpacks and follow me outside. "Cool," said a student in the back. "Can I take my coffee along?" asked another. "Bring whatever you wish. We are walking philosophers today. We will prove we can walk and think at the same time. Okay, boys and girls, remember the rules from elementary school: watch where you walk and don't trip over one another and be careful crossing streets. That's the first lesson of any philosophical school."

Before we headed outside, I held up a painting by Raphael and asked them to come up and look at it. The painting was called The School of Athens, and it was the painter's imaginative representation of what he thought the early schools of philosophy might have looked like. The students picked out the important elements immediately without my having to explain anything. They saw not a lecturer speaking to students seated in rows of chairs, but rather a number of small groups meeting, some seated, some standing, a few sitting on the floor. They also noted the sky overhead, making them aware students were not in an enclosed room. "It looks like organized chaos," one student comments. "It looks like what we do in our class," said another.

As we walked down the stairs and outside I told the students the stories of some of the first schools of philosophy in ancient Greece, especially the school of

A Teacher, His Students, and the Great Questions of Life

Epicurus where there was a garden where students could sit or walk and converse. "Plato also started a school, the Academy, as did Aristotle in Athens, which he called the Lyceum. Each of these were the models for a a liberal arts education today. These early philosophers understood that having a garden or a path to walk, to sit and talk along the way, was essential to a trained mind. And that's why we are taking a walk outside so I can show you what philosophy students built a few years ago."

I asked everyone to walk and not talk, asking them to remember the advice of their first teacher about the need to stop, look and listen before crossing a street. "It's the best advice you'll get about how best to live. Most of us frantically stay on the go and never slow down to look or listen. The first rule of life is to take care of yourself because no one else will. That's not selfish; it's self-preservation. Too many of us try to take care of everyone else and lose ourselves in the process. So let's just walk quietly, looking and listening."

All that could be heard were the patter of shoes on the pavement and the tapping of shoes on the pathway until we headed down a small hillside and stopped. We were near the river. "Listen for a minute to the river and ask yourself what it teaches you." The students were silent for a moment until I told them there were no correct answers, only what they felt the river was teaching them about how best to live. And then their comments flowed as the river.

"Just keep on moving."

"Go over and around any obstacles you find in your path in order to reach your goal."

"The water comes from the sky and goes back to it, no beginning nor end."

What Is Time?

"Water is the key to all life and it takes many forms—ponds and streams and rivers and the ocean."

"The river is full of life but it's often under the surface."

"Keep moving."

"If you just look and listen, that may be enough."

I let their words sink in as we stood quietly by for a few minutes before I walked further down the path to where there was a stone circle around which were trees and plants and boulders on which to sit.

"This simple garden was planned and planted by philosophy students some years ago after seeing a painting by Raphael of what he imagined the schools of philosophy of ancient Athens might have been—small groups of people sitting and standing but in an outside space with the blue sky overhead. The students wondered why we sat in a classroom with chairs lined up to face the front and shades drawn to block light from outside. They began at that point to dream of an outside space where students might walk to sit quietly or talk, surrounded by trees and the sound of the nearby river. So, here is the simple garden they planned. But that's not the end of the story. A few weeks after the garden was created, somebody came in, tore up the plants and the young trees, and overturned the bench. It was disheartening but the students decided not to be overcome. They felt they were in some kind of cosmic struggle between the forces of creation and destruction, and in a way they really were. So they raised money and bought new plants and one of the students arranged for her father to bring large rocks and boulders from a company he owned to the hill above the garden, where we would roll them down and up another small incline as places to sit.

A Teacher, His Students, and the Great Questions of Life

The day the rocks and boulders were delivered during our class time, the students went outside and in groups of four or five took turns pushing them down one hill and up another until they had arranged them in circles around the garden. I hadn't planned to say anything, but as we sat down, it dawned on me that we had recreated one of my favorite myths, recounted in Albert Camus' story about the myth of Sisyphus. In the original myth, Sisyphus is forced to roll a boulder up a hill, only when nearing the top to have it roll back down again; he then repeats the same action again and again. Camus uses this story to illustrate the absurdity of the human condition, but also the understanding that the struggle itself may be enough to make Sisyphus happy and by inference, us.

The students were quiet after I told the story, reflecting deeply as I urged them to do from time to time. Finally one of them, often the quietest during class time, spoke out. He had come from a difficult upbringing, his father incarcerated and his mother a recovering drug addict. He had grown up on the city streets and been in trouble with school officials and the police more than once. And yet someone somewhere had planted in him a desire to be more than others predicted and he had finished high school and come back to college to take night classes while working as a clerk in a local store. It was as if a light went on in his head and he blurted out: "I get it. Each one of us is Sisyphus. Like him I just have to keep on heading uphill even when the boulder falls back because that's what it means to be alive—keep on climbing." I knew he spoke for a lot of students in that class, many having dropped out of high school due to pregnancy, others struggling to survive growing up in poor, single parent families, still others working at low wages trying to

What Is Time?

advance their careers. No one said more as we got up and walked back to the classroom, but I felt he had touched a common chord. A light had gone on in his mind and others knew it.

A few years after this episode and after I had left teaching at this college, I returned to the place where the meditation garden had been built. The flowers and trees had been pulled out. The boulders on which students sat were gone, as was the stone bench. Papers, needles and cigarette butts covered the ground. I sat on a remaining wall and thought what the river taught now was that everything is transitory, nothing lasts, and all we have are brief moments of light and insight before the darkness returns. But what I remembered most of all was their insistence on not letting the destructive forces win. The garden was not the product; the students were.

When new students arrive in their first (and probably last) philosophy class because they need a few humanities credits to fulfill their graduation requirements, I know they have little idea what to expect. I usually try to arrive early and sit in the back of the room, a cell phone in my hand, the way most students sit in classrooms these days. I realize with my white hair, I may not look like a typical student, but what's typical these days anyway? Students in my classes are more diverse than many of the neighborhoods they live in or the congregations they attend, if they attend any congregation at all. Most consider themselves "spiritual" without being "religious," a topic we explore later when we study the philosophy of religion (a hint: religion comes from the Latin and means that which binds together; spiritual, also from the Latin, means breath or life).

I sit and wait for the class to start. A few students laugh or chatter among themselves; others are quiet, awaiting teacher's arrival. I practice what I teach and remain quiet, listening. Their comments help me to learn about their expectations. "So what the hell is philosophy anyway?" Another student says: "I have no idea. It's probably boring." Another looks at her cell phone (did you ever notice how few newer classrooms have clocks on the walls these days, another sign of the times?): "So how long are we supposed to wait before we leave?" A fourth holds up one of the assigned books: "Man, this book is less than a hundred pages. My sociology text is four hundred pages and costs nearly two hundred dollars."

I wait a few minutes after the official time for the class to begin and move slowly to the front of the room. "Welcome to philosophy, which is supposed to be about learning how to think more clearly and live more deeply, and I know it scares the hell out of some of you because you think it's going to be very abstract, even boring. So here is your first lesson: You are the textbook and you carry it with you at all times. So here in this room while we are locked up together for weeks, bring yourself and stay aware. That's the first rule of life anyway: Show up."

"Anyone have any questions?" No one responds. "You will bring many questions over our time together. It's called the Socratic method of learning. We'll wrestle with the questions together. Some students think of this kind of classroom experience as organized chaos. It is both chaotic but organized. So before you get comfortable in your chairs, we're going to talk a short walk. Leave your

What Is Time?

backpacks here. I will lock the door. Just bring yourself for our orientation to philosophy."

This time we walk down a city street. I ask only that they pay attention to what they hear, see, and especially feel. We walk quietly, slowly. From time to time, I pause. Sometimes I point, perhaps to a squirrel racing or a bird flying overhead. Soon a few of them begin pointing to other things they observe, a cloud formation or a man walking his dog.

I begin with a walking exercise, no blackboard, screen or barriers between myself and the students. It's up close and personal, no artificial barriers between us, a participatory sport in other words, the way it works best since the days when philosophers roamed the streets looking for an honest person.

"So, let's play the Socratic game, boys and girls. Here's the first question: What do you feel right now?"

No one responds at first, but then the responses come.

"A little nervous. I live in the suburbs and what I read about the city is drugs and muggings."

"I feel anxious. Not sure what I expect."

"I feel strange. I'm not used to walking down a street with a group of people."

"Feels like just another day to me," said one older student as we turned down a side alley. "I grew up on this street and still live here, and walk to the bus stop every day to get to classes."

Another student remarked about the broken bottles and trash everywhere. "Look at the houses around here. Some are boarded up and a lot of windows have been broken."

"I try to pick trash up whenever I leave in the morning, but it feels hopeless. By the time I get home there's more everywhere," said the student who lived on the block.

"Just like the myth of Sisyphus," I said, launching into the ancient story of the character who pushed a boulder up a hill, only to find that nearing the top it rolled back down. I asked them if any felt like Sisyphus and what they would advise him to do.

"I know I feel that way. I get tired of pushing the boulder and there are days when I just want to quit, but I know if I do, nothing will happen."

"So why not get others to help push the boulder over the top?" someone asked. "I mean, seems to me that we live in a culture where you're supposed to handle everything alone. Maybe if we learned to work together," we could get more accomplished.

"Look at that!" One student stopped and pointed to a small garden at the end of the alley. There was no graffiti on the walls and a few plants and benches were inside. The students stopped. "Hey, let's stop and sit." one suggested. "Yeah, it's like an oasis."

I had come prepared. I once gave a speech before a student organization and offered them five simple rules for living—and put them on a bookmark which I copied and handed out, thinking at least they might remember something I said and, if not, have a way to mark places in books they were reading. I handed the bookmark and suggested they read it and sit quietly for a few minutes.

1. *Keep it simple (it will get complex all by itself).*

2. *Know yourself (many conspire to take this away from you).*

3. *Be kind to yourself and others (somebody has to)*

4. *Seemingly small things matter most (there are no small things).*
5. *Take care of your soul (even if you don't believe you have one).*

I tried not to check my watch, but the more I thought about the passing time, the longer it seemed. I finally looked at my watch and realized we had been sitting still for five minutes. "Okay," I said softly, let's get back to class."

"Do we have to go?"

"Okay, not yet. Take a few more minutes to sit quietly," I responded, taking a deep breath.

The students sat quietly for longer than I thought possible. Some had their eyes closed while others seemed mesmerized by the design on the wall of a house next to the garden which showed young children planting flowers.

We walked back to the classroom. No one spoke until we neared the building, but one student said:

"Can we go there again? That was fun."

I was going to respond to the student that one of the faculty with more advanced degrees than fleas on my cats had cornered me one day to complain that one of my students had said how much she enjoyed the course she was taking from me and didn't I understand "learning is not supposed to be fun but serious?" But her comment made more sense to me than my learned colleague. I might have responded to him that I had had to deal with students in his class who were terrified of her and I didn't believe that was the best motivation for helping students learned. But I smiled and was grateful for her comment.

A Teacher, His Students, and the Great Questions of Life

We stood near the semi-circle wall of the meditation garden philosophy students had helped to create and sustain a year ago. Trees and plants were pulled out again. Boulders students had rolled down a hill to serve as sitting places had been moved and dumped into the nearby river. Cigarette butts, needles, and beer cans were tossed around the garden. "What a mess," one student said quietly as we stood silently and observed the destruction. The only sound were wind chimes students had placed high in trees. "At least something wasn't destroyed," one student said. I tried to think of something to say, but no words came out of my mouth. A few students began to pick up trash, but soon gave up realizing there was too much and it was scattered everywhere. I turned and walked away and others followed.

"Why do people do something like that?" a student said as we returned to the classroom. "I suppose they just like to destroy things," said another. "It's just like my neighborhood, " said another student. "We tried to pick up papers and trash that people threw around, but after a while we came to realize that no matter how hard we tried, the trash kept piling up. I finally gave up and moved away."

It took most of the class time reflecting on what we had just witnessed in the garden, but concluded with students saying they wanted to spend time later that day to clear up the mess. "I guess that's why we are here," said an older student. "We're here to clear up the messes others leave, but I just wish they didn't make them in the first place." The next time the class met they insisted we return to the garden where new plants had been put in and the trash picked up. "It's not as it used to be but it's like a statement about refusing to accept messes," said a student

What Is Time?

I knew had escaped from domestic abuse. "Yeah, but just understand the mess will be back tomorrow."

I was thinking about the college meditation garden and my own this morning as I looked in my backyard. All I could think to myself was what a mess it had become since I failed to take care of it. The fall had arrived, leaves were changing color, and the flowers in my garden were overrun with weeds and clinging vines. I let the garden go because a few months before I had tried to remove weeds, only to discover I had unwittingly grabbed poison ivy and was now suffering.

In a very real way, the garden in a metaphor for most of our lives. We try to plant beautiful flowers, but without caring for them weeds overtake and sometimes like clinging vines choke the life out. It takes vigilance, regular care, getting rid of weeds, and water and sunlight.

Which brings me back to my students who, like a garden, require care. Many have gone through harsh life experiences. I am sometimes surprised to learn about their lives. I see the classroom as a place where students bring themselves and in which they are given time to reflect on their lives, whether through keeping a journal or compiling their "book of life" (a single page on which they jot down items in their lives based on seven year chapters) and sharing it with others. Without formal lectures or videos, I have learned to trust that given permission, students yearn for a place to share their stories, learn from others, and often find ways to live better.

Let me share with you a story about one student ("Laura" rather than her real name) to illustrate the notion that where once philosophy in ancient times had been seen as a therapy, a way of clearing the mind and soul, it had become domesticated in modern times to be one subject taught among others.

Laura entered the introductory philosophy class the first time and sat in the back of the room. What I usually do the first class is have students rearrange the chairs into a circle so rather than looking at me or the screen on the front wall, they were forced to look at others. I then pulled my chair to be part of the circle. Laura still kept quiet for the first weeks, until one day she approached me after class and confessed she had been reading Kierkegaard and Rumi on her own for years and now that her three children were "out of diapers," as he phrased it, she had started college, something she had delayed.

When I asked her what subject she was studying," she replied almost apologetically: "Myself. I want to be a writer." Most students would have responded they wanted to study a subject to prepare them for a career, but only a few in my experience would have dared to confess that becoming a writer was their goal.

I tried to remain calm, as if wanting to be a writer were akin to desiring to be a computer programmer. "So, why a writer?"

She thought for a moment. "Not sure why, except that I've always felt I had something to say. My life's been a mess up until now, so maybe writing can help me figure out why and what's the next chapter all about?"

I ask students to do exercises that have some bearing on their lives. Each student creates a book of his or her life in which they divide their lives into seven year chapters and jot down notes about what they remember for each chapter, then share as much as they wish in a small group. I also give each one a journal and ask them to enter something into it each while the class meets, even if

What Is Time?

it is a sentence or two or drawing. Most of the students have never kept journals not thought about their lives as a book with chapters. They groan when I tell them they must write long hand in the journal. I remember one student complaining she thought she had forgotten how to write that way. My rationale was that by taking the time to write long hand they might also slow down and learn how to think more clearly.

Over our time together I watched Laura discover herself and her calling. I once said to her that having a calling was different from having a job. A job was something you did to earn money; a calling was something you felt you had to do and when you found it, you knew this was why you were put on earth.

"I don't know what I will do for a job, but I know what I will do for a living," Laara wrote in an essay.

In her papers she told her life story, and when she could, learned how to share them in a small group. She had been abused by a father, raised by a mother who spent time in and out of addiction treatment facilities, and sexually involved with a series of men who took advantage of her need for attention, and eventually spending time herself in an addiction treatment program. Pregnant in her teens, married to someone who abused her verbally, and now with three children, she had decided at some point she needed a new direction. For some reason, she heard about the community college and decided to start, one course at a time. My philosophy course was her first.

I am often surprised and amazed at stories like Laura's, of people who have hit rock bottom and somehow found a way out. I sometimes marvel at their courage and say to myself when I witness them that this is why I love being a teacher, a witness to their lives. There are many

A Teacher, His Students, and the Great Questions of Life

students who fit this narrative, and, I know, perhaps an equal number I cannot reach or who have chosen other paths of self-destruction. It is being present to hear their stories that confirms my commitment to being a teacher. I am no role model for sure, but when I hear their stories, I know myself better, that I have been there, done that, and grown.

I remember once that a student asked me to fill in my response to an incomplete sentence I had given the class to complete: I am here to_____. Without thinking, I wrote the same response Viktor Frankl supplied to someone who asked him the same question: "I am here to help other people figure out why they are here."[*1] In writing this, I realized that being a teacher is really about relationships, about helping others but also helping yourself at the same time. It's another way to state the ancient admonition to love your neighbor as yourself.

When students first enter my classroom, they become quiet. Many try to hide in the back rows. Seldom does anyone sit in the first row. And when I arrive, everyone looks up and stares, wondering what will happen. They are accustomed to sitting in rows of chairs, all facing a screen where they can see my notes or videos.

The first thing I usually do is post a picture of Raphael's painting of what he envisioned to be the first school of philosophy in Athen. I ask them what they see. Many see small groups speaking with one another. A few see a person laying down. Someone notices the sky above the space. I let them know that this is painting that imagines what the earliest schools of philosophy were like over

---

1. Viktor E. Frankl: *Man's Search for Meaning*, Boston: Beacon Press, 2006, p. 165.)

What Is Time?

2,500 years ago in Athens. And then I suggest that we rearrange our meeting space to resemble that early school. Luckily, the chairs have wheels, and students soon follow the instructions, chairs often in a circle, people facing one another rather than the front screen.

"This is what I call learning space. We can see one another. Some students have called this organized chaos, and I guess it is. Learning is trying to form some order out of what seems chaos, whether in our classroom or your minds."

A student raises her hand. "Where did you learn to do that?" I ask. "Probably in first grade," she responds. I explain that in this class as we learn to listen, we will discover how to wait to speak until others are finished. "It's hard, I know. Most of us think of what we are going to respond to someone even before they are finished."

I then bring out one of my many props, a little stone, and tell the story. A friend gave one to me long ago as a way of disciplining oneself to really listen to others. He claimed it was given him by a Native American shaman, but I suspect he was the real source of the story he would tell each time he gave a stone to someone. I would use his words as I gave the stone to a student: "There's nothing magical or mystical about this stone. It's based on firm scientific principles. If you rub the stone, you will learn to pause before you speak and feel calm. Here's what I want you to do. Take the stone home tonight and put it under your pillow. Rub it before you go to sleep, and when you wake up in the morning you will feel relaxed and ready to face the new day. And you will laugh because either the stone worked or you know I pulled a fast one on you." I would then explain to the students that this was our listening stone. Whomever had it could talk while others listened. One could only talk when one had the stone.

The stone worked to help students listen. Each week a student would take the stone home. I joked that if lost, I would find where that student lived and come to the house to retrieve it. In all the years I've used this process, no one has ever lost the stone, though some confessed it made them fearful of doing so. I would then start a process I call check-ins, in which students could say whatever they wished to let others know about their week or anything else. It was a way of helping them to see they were the textbooks and their time to check in was their way of inviting others into their stories. Each person holding the stone was the only one permitted to talk; the others listened. Depending on the size of the class, some days no one had much to say; other days, many did, and it took some time to do so. But I bet that while most students wouldn't remember what I said, they would remember the stories told by others during check-ins—the time a student's mother had died the night before the class, the daughter arrested for drug possession, a child heading off to the first day of school. These were the real moments of lives, news that lasts.

I admit the chaotic part of class time could upset and frustrate some students who were more accustomed to sitting in rows of chairs facing the front where the teacher lectured or pointed to a screen. It was what I called the piggybank form of learning where a teacher assumes students are piggy banks with slits in the back of their heads into which information would be poured. Learning was supposed to take place where that information was regurgitated at a later time on a multiple choice test. The kind of learning in an organized chaos setting is more difficult to measure, though I designed some different ways to measure it. For example, I had students keep daily journals and later reflect on them. I had them writing ethical wills, saying what they valued and wanted to leave behind. I even had each one write a letter to himself or herself, which I never read but mailed to them months later.

I reduced my syllabus one page with only two objectives: to help students learn how to think more clearly, and to help them learn how to live more deeply. Seemed like basic goals of learning to me, but often unfamiliar to students. The purpose of being here, I would explain, is to grow a soul, a soul in the original meaning of the whole self—body, mind, and spirit. It's not just to get a job, I would continue, but to get a life. Aristotle's word of this goal, arete, always made sense to me—the purpose of a human life is to reach its full potential (in my case to think and live well).

After a few class sessions, students grow used to the seating arrangement and open dialog. Hands are not raised, but people seem to spend a few seconds before they speak, I let them know they are in charge of maintaining classroom discipline, and they do. If the discussion gets too heated, someone ask for time out to permit time for quiet reflection. If students arrive late for class, the other students all stand when he or she enters. They laugh. But no one is late a second time.

So what's my rationale for organized chaos? First I think many students live in chaos, and it is often not well organized. They seem literally besides themselves when they first enter the classroom, which is why I give them a few moments of quiet time before beginning, a discipline I hope they carry in their daily lives. My hope is to give them some simple ways to find order in their lives, perhaps what Robert Frost meant when he described poetry as a "momentary stay against confusion."

I remember one student who came to a first evening class and in the first half hour fell asleep, nodding his head every once in awhile. When it was time for a break, I went over to him and suggested we have a talk. It turned out he had been evicted from the apartment where he was staying with his sister, a drug user, and her supplier-boyfriend. This student had not eaten since grabbing a donut and coffee for breakfast. His life was spiraling out of control. I violated college policy and gave him a few dollars to get something to eat in the campus coffee shop. I walked downstairs with him and after he got a sandwich and carton of milk, we sat down in a corner and talked, mostly about how he could bring some order into his life. He said the first thing he needed to do was get out of his sister's apartment. He did that week and as the weeks passed, I noticed changes. He was more alert in class, participated in discussions, and would often stay after class to talk about his progress. While some might argue I was acting more like a counselor or social worker than teacher, I would argue that if self-knowledge is the heart of the philosophical journey, I was fulfilling my teacher role.

I know most students take their studies seriously, whether to get a high grade or later on a job. But silliness and laughter are also great wisdom teachers, helping us to let go of our egos long enough to discover something new. And playing games is one of the best ways to learn in a playful and even enjoyable way.

What Is Time?

If you doubt the wisdom of playful silliness as a way to learn, watch children. Don't observe them in a classroom setting where they are forced to sit in rows and raise hands if they want to speak. Rather, watch children during a break on the playground. They run and play and laugh. They seem to lose their self-awareness in the flow of the game. A teacher may monitor the play and even sometimes participate, but over all the children know best. And in the process they learn some important life lessons, such as how to work with a group, deal with a bully, get rid of excess energy in acceptable ways.

I admit to creating a playful environment in my classroom. I tell jokes, often at my expense to help them learn that if I don't take myself seriously it's okay for them as well. I go the back of the room and try to throw a rolled up paper ball into the trash can up front, letting them know my hero is Julius Erving ("Dr. J") of Philadelphia basketball fame. "Let's see if you can dunk like Dr. J.," one student challenges me. So I do. I run across the room and jump in the air to slam a ball of paper in the basket. The class erupts in applause and laughter.

I sometimes wonder what other faculty think of what they must think is unruly student behaviors. One time the teacher in the next classroom poked his head in and asked if we were okay because of the laughter he heard. I gave him a thumbs up gesture and after left, students told me he required them to sit in rows, take notes, and only speak after raising a hand. "It's the longest couple hours I've ever spent," said one student. "And I honestly don't remember anything from that course," another confessed.

We often play the dictionary game. It's an old game that doesn't require more than dictionary. I provide a word and students are first asked it they know what it means

A Teacher, His Students, and the Great Questions of Life

and, if not, to make up a definition they think will fool others. Meanwhile, I write the correct definition down. When everyone is done, the sheets are passed around and read and students vote on the definition they think is the right one. It always amuses that someone their definitions are better than the real ones and often require them to imagine new ones. It's also interesting that over weeks, students remember the words and definitions. When I choose words I try to find ones that are keys to the subjects we are studying. For example, I often use the word *Arete,* which is Aristotle's word for what he believes is the purpose of life—to flourish or become all one is capable of becoming. After the game, I ask students to think together about what they believe might be their purpose in living. Their thoughts are shared and often they realize that Aristotle had a point since his understanding mirrored theirs.

One time I used the word *Pooka* for the dictionary game and it led to some unintended consequences, which is what often happens in playful learning since one never really knows the sure outcome ahead of time. No one got close to the correct definition: a Pooka is a mischievous creature in mythology, often found in Irish tales. I mention the Pooka in the movie *Harvey* as an example. Of course, few of the students have seen this movie made long ago, so when they want to know more about Harvey I explain he is an eight-foot white rabbit that only the main character sees at first. I then take a cap with long white hairs out of my briefcase and show them Harvey. Okay, it is silly, but that's the reason I do it, figuring if I can act silly they will see it's okay.

One evening I talked about the Pooka, and put the ears on. One student, probably a Pooka himself, challenged

What Is Time?

me at the end of class to wear them out in the hallway as I left to get my car. Being a minor Pooka myself, I love challenges. So I put my ears on, grabbed my briefcase, walked out the door, down the hallway and into the large room where people gather. I did not know that that evening the college board of trustees was meeting and was quite surprised to see one of their professors with rabbit ears. I walked out as fast as I could, wondering what dire repercussions there might be. The next day, the administrator called me into his office. "One of the board members asked me last who was the professor with rabbit ears," he asked. He wasn't upset but he did say that he wished there had been professors like that when he was in college because most of the time he had been bored.

Life is simply too short to be bored when the universe is calling out to you to become all you are capable of being—laughter, tears, joy and sorrow.

Appendix

How to Use This Book with Small Groups

Keep it simple; it will get complex all by itself.

This book was intended to be used as a catalyst and resource for small groups to engage in dialog over the great questions of life. The educational setting for such groups might be high school or college courses in philosophy, groups in religious institutions, or small gatherings of people meeting informally at home or public locations to talk about the eleven questions in the book. The objective was to take philosophy into the public domain as it once was and provide places for people to come together to enjoy one another and the great ideas of the philosophical tradition.

The best advice in using this book to start a small group is this: Keep it simple; it will get complex all by itself. Here are some of the questions asked about creating and nurturing small philosophy groups and basic answers.

Appendix

How do I get started?

If you teach a course in philosophy or the great ideas, you can simply incorporate this book into your regular course offerings. I create many small groups in the courses I teach and use the questions in the book as a way for these groups to organize themselves. If you are a member of any religious institution this book might be used as a resource for religious education, both for adults and children and sometimes both together. It is also possible to create your own small group in the community (one such process is called the Socrates Café and information about this can be found on the web).

What's the major goal of this process?

The major goal is to bring people together to engage in dialog over the great questions of life. Long ago this was done in the earliest schools of Aristotle and Plato. Today this is done in educational or religious institutions or community settings. Part of the process is to introduce people not only to the great ideas but to each other, and to build a community of learners who grow by learning to listen learn, and respect one another.

What's the difference between dialog and discussion?

Socratic dialog is a term with a long history stretching back to ancient Greece. The easiest way to understand the differences between dialog and discussion is to think about the root meanings of each word. Dialog comes from a Latin word which means approximately "seeking the meaning through." Dialog requires active listening, the search for common ground, and the willingness to change one's mind if convinced. Discussion comes from the same root as the words percussion or concussion and often with the same results. Think of discussion as a tennis match with ideas hit across the net without taking the time to think much. Think of dialog as people listening to one another to seek a shared truth.

How's a group work?

I always suggest a group begin with two objectives: to get to know one another first and then to set the ground rules for each meeting. At the initial meeting, a group may simply go around and take some time to hear one another's stories. Then the group talks about their guidelines for behavior. Typical guidelines includes to listen to one another and not interrupt, to be respectful of what is said, to keep what is said within the group.

Who leads the group?

Someone there may already be the starting leader (teacher, professor, clergy person, etc.). Other times, outside of an institutional setting, a volunteer leader emerges and assumes responsibility for the first meeting. I believe shared leadership is important for this kind of small group process. At the first meeting, persons agree to take turns leading the group, which essentially means keeping them focused on the steps of the group process (see below, "Is there a suggested group process?").

Appendix

Is there a suggested group process?

I have found it's important to have a simple but regularly followed process or ritual for every meeting. Here's what I have found over time seems to work best:

1. Group leader for that meeting opens with a reading he or she has selected that may have something to do with question for that gathering.

2. Persons go around and check in with whatever they wish to say about their lives (option to pass always given). This is not a time for discussion, but simply checking in. I sometime use a stone ("the listening stone"), which is passed around with the understanding that only the person holding the stone may speak; the rest practice active listening.

3. The group leader then simply asks the question for that meeting (one of the eleven in the book), and opens up the session for dialog. At first meetings, persons may feel somewhat fearful of speaking and may need to be encouraged, but as the group grows to trust one another, the role of the leader may shift to making sure everyone has a chance to speak.

4. Near ending time, the group leader tries to summarize what people talked about, the next assigned question and reading in the book, and asks someone to volunteer to be the next leader (if no one volunteers, appoint someone).

How often and how long do meetings last?

If part of a high school, college or small group within a religious institution, groups should last about one typi-

Appendix

cal class period of 45-60 minutes. Teachers often use one question a week in small groups. If not in an institutional setting, usually groups last the same time limits, but in such settings often there are light refreshments after the meeting for those who want to hang around and talk. In community settings, the groups tend to meet one night a month for the eleven week duration. Often Wednesday evenings are chosen, though some groups may decide a breakfast meeting before people head off to work is best.

Are other books used?

No. The rationale for this is if other books are brought in, the gatherings tend to focus on the books, not one another. People may suggest books they feel others might be interested in reading. And it might be possible to think that after the small group completes all eleven questions, they might want to consider continuing in another form, such as a book discussion group. But the clear and simple mission of the small in the beginning is to engage in dialog over the eleven questions.

Where might such groups meet?

If you are in a educational or religious setting, you probably already have the place to meet. But if not, you can meet in one another's homes, in a community setting such as library or coffee shop. But where you meet should be relatively quiet and in a separate room or place where your dialog can remain private.

Appendix

Where can I get help?

Hopefully you won't need much because the mission and process are clear and simple. One website I have found useful is www.socratescafe.com It's not quite the same process I suggest here, but it's close and there is a clear summary of the Socratic process and examples of how this might work. If you want to check with me before you start, you can contact me at: drjohncmorgan@yahoo.com

www.ingramcontent.com/pod-product-compliance
Lightning Source LLC
Chambersburg PA
CBHW072142160426
43197CB00012B/2209